W9-CEC-345

Current
CONTROVERSIES

Antifa and the Radical Left

Other Books in the Current Controversies Series

Current
CONTROVERSIES

Antifa and the Radical Left

Eamon Doyle, Book Editor

GREENHAVEN
PUBLISHING

Published in 2019 by Greenhaven Publishing, LLC
353 3rd Avenue, Suite 255, New York, NY 10010

Articles in Greenhaven Publishing anthologies are often edited for length to meet page
requirements. In addition, original titles of these works are changed to clearly present
the main thesis and to explicitly indicate the author's opinion. Every effort is made to
ensure that Greenhaven Publishing accurately reflects the original intent of the authors.
Every effort has been made to trace the owners of the copyrighted material.

Cover image: Sheila Fitzgerald / Shutterstock.com

Library of Congress Cataloging-in-Publication Data

Names: Doyle, Eamon, editor.
Title: Antifa and the radical left / Eamon Doyle, book editor.
Description: First edition. | New York : Greenhaven Publishing, 2019. |
 Series: Current controversies | Includes bibliographical references and
 index. | Audience: Grades 9–12.
Identifiers: LCCN 2018028211| ISBN 9781534503847 (library bound) | ISBN
 9781534504554 (pbk.)
Subjects: LCSH: Antifa (Organisation) | Anti-fascist movements. |
 Anti-fascist movements—United States.
Classification: LCC JC481 .A573 2019 | DDC 320.53/30973—dc23
LC record available at https://lccn.loc.gov/2018028211

Manufactured in the United States

Website: http://greenhavenpublishing.com

Contents

Bonenberger examines the relationship between violence and political strategy in the context of the contemporary Left/Right divide in American politics. He argues that the Right's celebration of and preparedness for violence (including military service, gun ownership, belligerent political rhetoric, etc.) has afforded it a distinct strategic advantage over the Left.

No: It Is Counterproductive and Hypocritical to Use Violent and Anti-Democratic Tactics

D'Amato argues that comparisons between Left Wing and Right Wing violence rest on a false equivalency. In the former case, violence is used in a limited way to prevent the spread of inherently violent ideologies. In the latter, violence is used to quell opposition to an authoritarian political order based on such ideologies.

Foreword

"Controversy" is a word that has an undeniably unpleasant connotation. It carries a definite negative charge. Controversy can spoil family gatherings, spread a chill around classroom and campus discussion, inflame public discourse, open raw civic wounds, and lead to the ouster of public officials. We often feel that controversy is almost akin to bad manners, a rude and shocking eruption of that which must not be spoken or thought of in polite, tightly guarded society. To avoid controversy, to quell controversy, is often seen as a public good, a victory for etiquette, perhaps even a moral or ethical imperative.

Yet the studious, deliberate avoidance of controversy is also a whitewashing, a denial, a death threat to democracy. It is a false sterilizing and sanitizing and superficial ordering of the messy, ragged, chaotic, at times ugly processes by which a healthy democracy identifies and confronts challenges, engages in passionate debate about appropriate approaches and solutions, and arrives at something like a consensus and a broadly accepted and supported way forward. Controversy is the megaphone, the speaker's corner, the public square through which the citizenry finds and uses its voice. Controversy is the life's blood of our democracy and absolutely essential to the vibrant health of our society.

Our present age is certainly no stranger to controversy. We are consumed by fierce debates about technology, privacy, political correctness, poverty, violence, crime and policing, guns, immigration, civil and human rights, terrorism, militarism, environmental protection, and gender and racial equality. Loudly competing voices are raised every day, shouting opposing opinions, putting forth competing agendas, and summoning starkly different visions of a utopian or dystopian future. Often these voices attempt to shout the others down; there is precious little listening and considering among the cacophonous din. Yet listening and considering, too, are essential to the health of a democracy. If controversy is democracy's lusty lifeblood, respectful listening and careful thought are its higher faculties, its brain, its conscience.

Current Controversies does not shy away from or attempt to hush the loudly competing voices. It seeks to provide readers with as wide and representative as possible a range of articulate voices on any given controversy of the day, separates each one out to allow it to be heard clearly and fairly, and encourages careful listening to each of these well-crafted, thoughtfully expressed opinions, supplied by some of today's leading academics, thinkers, analysts, politicians, policy makers, economists, activists, change agents, and advocates. Only after listening to a wide range of opinions on an issue, evaluating the strengths and weaknesses of each argument, assessing how well the facts and available evidence mesh with the stated opinions and conclusions, and thoughtfully and critically examining one's own beliefs and conscience can the reader begin to arrive at his or her own conclusions and articulate his or her own stance on the spotlighted controversy.

This process is facilitated and supported in each Current Controversies volume by an introduction and chapter overviews that provide readers with the essential context they need to begin engaging with the spotlighted controversies, with the debates surrounding them, and with their own perhaps shifting or nascent opinions on them. Chapters are organized around several key questions that are answered with diverse opinions representing all points on the political spectrum. In its content, organization, and methodology, readers are encouraged to determine the authors' point of view and purpose, interrogate and analyze the various arguments and their rhetoric and structure, evaluate the arguments' strengths and weaknesses, test their claims against available facts and evidence, judge the validity of the reasoning, and bring into clearer, sharper focus the reader's own beliefs and conclusions and how they may differ from or align with those in the collection or those of classmates.

Research has shown that reading comprehension skills improve dramatically when students are provided with compelling, intriguing, and relevant "discussable" texts. The subject matter of these collections could not be more compelling, intriguing, or urgently relevant to today's students and the world they are poised to inherit. The anthologized articles also provide the basis for stimulating, lively, and passionate classroom debates. Students who are compelled to anticipate objections to their own argument and identify the flaws in those of an opponent read more carefully, think more critically, and steep themselves in relevant context, facts, and information more thoroughly. In short, using discussable text of the kind provided by every single volume in the Current Controversies series encourages close reading, facilitates reading comprehension, fosters research, strengthens critical thinking, and greatly enlivens and energizes classroom discussion and participation. The entire learning process is deepened, extended, and strengthened.

If we are to foster a knowledgeable, responsible, active, and engaged citizenry, we must provide readers with the intellectual, interpretive, and critical-thinking tools and experience necessary to make sense of the world around them and of the all-important debates and arguments that inform it. We must encourage them not to run away from or attempt to quell controversy but to embrace it in a responsible, conscientious, and thoughtful way, to sharpen and strengthen their own informed opinions by listening to and critically analyzing those of others. This series encourages respectful engagement with and analysis of current controversies and competing opinions and fosters a resulting increase in the strength and rigor of one's own opinions and stances. As such, it helps readers assume their rightful place in the public square and provides them with the skills necessary to uphold their awesome responsibility—guaranteeing the continued and future health of a vital, vibrant, and free democracy.

Introduction

> *"Of all recent social struggles, anti-fascism faces perhaps the most difficult road toward establishing itself as an extension of over a century of struggle against white supremacy, patriarchy, and authoritarianism."*
>
> —*Mark Bray*, Antifa: The Anti-Fascist Handbook

The year 2016 was a grim one for the American Left. Many found that their preferred candidate for president—Bernie Sanders—came within striking distance of clinching the Democratic Party's nomination but ultimately fell short. And then Donald Trump, who many liberals perceived as incorporating openly nativist and authoritarian themes into his official campaign and policy platforms, was elected President of the United States. Trump's victory sent shockwaves through American liberals, who were still reeling from the sensory assault of a highly acrimonious and controversial campaign. This sequence of crushing disappointments contributed to demoralization among the Left—but also to new pockets of energy and resistance.[1] The protest/counter-protest movement known as Antifa is one example.

For a variety of reasons, Antifa tends to resist easy categorization and description. The movement has no central organizational structure and, because many members of Antifa-aligned groups wear masks to demonstrations and avoid interacting with the media, participation is often anonymous. The word itself is an abbreviation of "Anti-Fascism," which has been used to describe a variety of groups and activities since the ascent of Fascism in Europe in the 1930s. But in the context of contemporary American politics, it typically refers to a loosely organized network of liberal and Leftist protest groups that employ aggressive demonstration tactics to confront, challenge, intimidate, and silence perceived Fascist or Far Right ideologues. *CNN*'s Jessica Suerth offers the following description of the movement:

> [Antifa] is used to define a broad group of people whose political beliefs lean toward the left—often the far left—but do not conform with the Democratic Party platform. The group doesn't have an official leader or headquarters, although groups in certain states hold regular meetings. Antifa positions can be hard to define, but many members support oppressed populations and protest the amassing of wealth by corporations and elites. Some employ radical or militant tactics to get their message across.[2]

From a purely strategic perspective, the Antifa network's decentralized structure affords significant benefits—and a number of drawbacks as well. It has contributed to the groups' agility and rapid response capabilities, but it has also fostered confusion about the groups' motives, alienated moderates, and opened the door to competition and infighting among its various factions. Dhruv Devulapalli of the *Berkeley Political Review* assesses the movement's strategic position and organizational structure in the following passage:

> US Antifa groups have adopted the "no platform" policies of their European counterparts, whereby they do not take a broad political stance in order to unify anti-fascist activists who may not agree on all political issues. As a result, the Antifa movement has many different, generally leftist, factions: communists, socialist democrats, and anarchists. [...] Since the group itself doesn't have a platform, it's unclear what its various factions will do in the future, or what their objectives will be after its goals are met. Will the group enter the mainstream once the political

scenario is more conducive to their policies, or will the anarchist factions take over and continue to oppose any government?[3]

In addition to the question of Antifa's future, there is no consensus as to the effectiveness of its tactics. In fact, its presence on the political scene has contributed to infighting in the Democratic Party and among liberals in general.

Some on the Left argue that the threat posed by resurgent Fascist and Far Right ideologies in America—a development they take to be represented by President Trump's election, the rapid growth of the Alt-Right community and its media ecosystem, and recent public rallies and open demonstrations by avowed White Nationalists—is sufficiently grave to render violent resistance permissible or even necessary. But strategists in the Democratic Party are concerned that Antifa's tactics could alienate moderates and centrist-minded conservatives and squander an opportunity to attract some of these voters, many of whom do not support President Trump, in upcoming elections.

Additionally, centrist-minded liberals have pointed out the hypocrisy of employing violent and repressive tactics to resist a movement that one is rejecting on the basis of its violent and repressive nature. The political scientist Andrew E. Busch exemplifies this criticism:

> The radical movement, encompassing Antifa, Black Lives Matter, and others, represents a broad, even amorphous, collection of groups and individuals, and there is not a uniform view among them. It undoubtedly includes many individuals who sincerely believe they are fighting against fascism, racism, or police brutality. However, one can construct a composite of today's radical Left and test it against our checklist of historical fascism. What one finds is that, on balance, today's radicals have much more in common with fascism than most analysts have recognized […] Where does that leave us? At the moment, both white nationalists and radicals are carnival sideshows, aberrations in a country that still, by and large, values peace and freedom. Nevertheless, we are in a place few would have

expected a decade ago. One set of newly bold extremists includes self-conscious national socialists as well as other overlapping forces driven by white identity politics. Though covered with a façade of egalitarianism, an alternative extreme has much more in common with the tactics and even philosophical framework of fascism than even it understands. Both groups of extremists seem determined to provoke the other into more and more serious confrontations. A feckless president has contributed to polarization by giving comfort to the alt-right—as his equally feckless predecessor did by endorsing BLM—and seems at a loss when confronted with the consequences. And an increasingly concerned and leaderless center witnesses what looks to some like the unraveling of their country, and are uncertain what to do about it. Weimar America? Not yet. [...] But one fears we are closer to the beginning than to the end of this story. [4]

The Democratic Party and the Left in America are faced with a conundrum. More energy and more aggressive activism from Antifa-aligned groups have aggravated ideological and cultural fractures in the traditional American liberal coalition. For this reason, the specter of Antifa will loom large in upcoming congressional elections in 2018 and especially the presidential primary in 2020, elections likely to be among the most consequential in the Democratic Party's history. Understanding this elusive movement is key to understanding the present moment in American politics, and the viewpoints presented in *Current Controversies: Antifa and the Radical Left* will help elucidate it.

Notes

1. Laura Sydell, "On Both the Left and Right, Trump Is Driving New Political Engagement," NPR Online, March 3, 2017. https://www.npr.org/2017/03/03/518261347/on-both-left-and-right-trump-is-driving-new-political-engagement.

2. Jessica Suerth, "What Is Antifa?" CNN, August 17, 2017. https://www.cnn.com/2017/08/14/us/what-is-antifa-trnd/index.html.

3. "Antifa: A New Political Resistance?" by Dhruv Devulapalli, *Berkeley Political Review,* March 23, 2017.

4. "Fascism in America?" essay originally appeared in the *Claremont Review of Books,* by Andrew E. Busch, September 12, 2017.

Chapter 1

Does Antifa Endorse a Specific Positive Political Ideology?

The Complicated History of Antifa Groups

Loren Balhorn

Loren Balhorn is a writer and contributing editor to Jacobin
Magazine *in Berlin. He is also an anti-war activist and a member
of the German democratic socialist party Die Linke.*

The origins of the word "antifa"—shorthand for decentralized,
militant street activism associated with its own aesthetic and
subculture—might be murky to most readers. Even in Germany,
few know much about the popular forms of antifascist resistance
that coined the term.

The movement's short but inspiring political legacy proved
too uncomfortable for both Cold War-era German states, and
was ignored in schools and mainstream history. Today its legacy
is almost entirely lost to the Left.

Out of the Ruins

By 1945, Hitler's Third Reich lay physically destroyed and politically
exhausted. Basic civil society ceased to function in many areas, as
the Nazi grip on power faltered and regime supporters, particularly
in the middle- and upper classes, realized that Hitler's "final
victory" was a fantasy.

On the Left, many Communists and Social Democrats had
either been outright murdered by the Nazis, or died in the ensuing
war. The unimaginable human and material destruction wrought
by Nazi rule killed millions and turned German society upside
down, decimating the labor movement and murdering most of
the country's Jewish population. Millions who had supported or at
least acquiesced to the regime—including many workers and even
some former socialists—now faced a new beginning in unknown
political terrain.

"The Lost History of Antifa," by Loren Balhorn, jacobinmag.com, May 8, 2017. Reprinted
by permission.

Yet despite its failure to stop Hitler in 1933 and veritable dismantling in subsequent years, Germany's socialist labor movement and its decidedly progressive traditions outlived Hitler in the factories of its industrial cities, and began gathering up the fragments as soon as open political activity became possible. As historian Gareth Dale describes:

> Of all sectors of the population, it was industrial workers in the major towns that showed the greatest immunity to Nazism. Many trade unionists and socialists were able to maintain their traditions and beliefs, at least in some form, through the Nazi era. A courageous minority, including some 150,000 Communists, took part in illegal resistance. Wider layers avoided danger but were able to keep labour movement values and memories alive amongst groups of friends, in workplaces and on housing estates.

These groups, oftentimes launched from the aforementioned housing estates, were generally called "Antifaschistische Ausschüsse," "Antifaschistische Kommittees," or the now famous "Antifaschistische Aktion"—"Antifa" for short. They drew on the slogans and orientation of the prewar united front strategy, adopting the word "Antifa" from a last-ditch attempt to establish a cross-party alliance between Communist and Social Democratic workers in 1932. The alliance's iconic logo, devised by Association of Revolutionary Visual Artists members Max Keilson and Max Gebhard, has been since become one of the Left's most well-known symbols.

After the war, Antifas varied in size and composition across the former Reich, now divided into four zones of occupation, and developed in interaction with the local occupying power. Emerging seemingly overnight in dozens of cities, most formed immediately after Allied forces arrived, while some such as the group in Wuppertal "liberated" themselves in street battles with Hitler loyalists before the Allies could.

Pivotally, these circles were not spontaneous instances of solidarization between traumatized war survivors, but the product of Social Democratic Party (SPD) and Communist Party (KPD) veterans reactivating prewar networks. Albrecht Lein reports that the core of the Braunschweig Antifa was made up of KPD and SPD members in their forties and fifties who had avoided the front, though Catholic workers' organizations and other forces were also involved.

The Antifa groups numbered between several hundred and several thousand active members in most cities, while the openly decried lack of youth involvement can be ascribed to twelve years of Nazi education and socialization, which annihilated the once widespread proletarian-socialist attitude among most young Germans. Though the material needs of war and reconstruction incorporated women into economic life in new ways, the male dominance characteristic of German society at the time was also reflected in the Antifa movement, which consisted largely (but not entirely) of men.

Antifas tended to focus on a combination of hunting down Nazi criminals and underground Nazi partisans (the so-called "Werewolves") and practical concerns affecting the general population. Braunschweig's Antifa, for example, printed a twelve-point program demanding, among other things, the removal of Nazis from all administrative bodies and their immediate replacement with "competent antifascists," liquidation of Nazi assets to provide for war victims, emergency laws to prosecute local fascists, and the reestablishment of the public health-care service. Typical of an organization led by socialists and thus keenly aware of the need for print media as an organizing medium, the program's twelfth and final point consisted bluntly of a "Daily newspaper."

Although surviving records indicate that many Antifas were dominated by the KPD, the political mood in the early months was far from the "Third Period" adventurism of the late Weimar period. Across the board, local Antifas were motivated by a desire to learn from the mistakes of 1933 and build a non-sectarian labor movement bridging divisions. This was buoyed by a widespread sense at the war's end that the horrors of Nazism had been a result of the instability and inequality of capitalism, and that a new, egalitarian economic system was needed for the postwar order.

Demands for nationalization of industry and other left-wing policies were widespread. Even the forced marriage between KPD and SPD into the Socialist Unity Party (SED) in the Soviet zone drew on this sentiment and recruited many former oppositionists in the first year. In British-occupied Hamburg, a joint KPD-SPD action committee convened in July 1945 with broad support from their respective memberships to declare:

> The will to merge into a powerful political party lives in the hearts of the millions of supporters of the once warring German workers' parties as the most meaningful outcome of their shared suffering. This desire is deeply etched into all of the surviving prisoners from the concentration camps, prisons, and Gestapo institutions.

The rest of the document consisted of practical demands around which to unite Hamburg's fragmented labor movement.

Antifas enjoyed varying degrees of success depending on the composition of the local movement and the amount of leeway allowed to them by occupying powers. Despite forming outside of the Allied administration and pushing forward popular de-Nazification policies against occupying forces who sought reconciliation with the old authorities, they were in no position to contest Allied hegemony and represented militant minorities at best.

The southwestern industrial city of Stuttgart, for example, was fortunate enough to be involved in territorial maneuvering between the United States and France, which occupied the city preemptively. Keen to avoid civil unrest and thus give the Americans a pretext to take it back, French authorities allowed Stuttgart's antifascists considerable leeway in dismantling the Nazi-era German Labor Front (DAF), rebuilding shop-floor organization in the factories, and organizing the population in cross-party antifascist alliances.

Stuttgart is also noteworthy for the presence of the Communist Party (Opposition), or KPO. This group around former KPD leaders August Thalheimer and Heinrich Brandler had recruited a large number of the city's mid-level KPD factory activists and functionaries following that party's ultra-left turn in 1929. The KPO's vocal advocacy for an anti-Nazi front of all workers' organizations in the run-up to 1933 allowed it to consolidate a small but considerable base of experienced Communist cadre repulsed by the Stalinization of their party.

Although never a mass organization and only a shadow of its former self after the war, what remained of the KPO had a decisive influence over Stuttgart's metal workers' union for several years and was able to play a role in the factories. These activists and others provided the city with a core of capable militants who understood, through experience, the need to unite workers on a cross-party basis around basic social demands.

Like everywhere else in Germany, Stuttgart's Antifa movement was soon neutralized and diverted back into the old divisions between SPD and KPD, but the city's rebellious tradition and penchant for unity in action would reemerge in 1948, when widespread anger at drastic price rises triggered a citywide general strike that encompassed 79 percent of the workforce and spread to several other localities.

Overdetermined

The Antifa movement faced an almost impossible situation in 1945. The country lay in ruins in every sense imaginable, and had gone through a phase of destruction, brutality, and wanton murder unprecedented in scale.

The Antifa's predicament was by and large "overdetermined," in the sense that historical forces beyond their control would ultimately seal their fate. These socialists and antifascists, though numbering in the tens of thousands across the country, could not have been expected to provide a plausible political alternative to the overwhelming might of the Cold War.

Germany in 1945 was set to become the staging ground for the longest geopolitical confrontation in modern history, and there was no way the fragments of a shattered socialist movement could have influenced developments in any meaningful way. Nevertheless, statements and documents from the time reveal thousands of determined antifascists and socialists, keenly aware of the unprecedented nature of their historical moment and putting forward a political perspective for what remained of the country's working class.

Although their numbers were comparatively and regrettably few given the movement's former glory, their existence refutes the notion that the prewar German left was entirely destroyed by Nazism. Hitler certainly broke the back of German socialism, but West Germany's postwar prosperity laced with anti-Communist paranoia would finally bury what remained of the country's radical prewar traditions.

Albrecht Lein recounts how the incredibly difficult conditions facing the Antifa also necessarily restricted their political perspective. Though they attracted thousands of socialists and were soon bolstered by returning Communists and other political prisoners from the concentration camps, briefly becoming the dominant political force in cities like Braunschweig, they were unable to offer a political road out of the country's social misery.

Lein argues that the labor movement's failure to defeat Hitler and the fact that Germany had required liberation from without drove antifascists to a largely reactive policy, vigorously pursuing former Nazi officials and purging society of collaborators, but neglecting to build a plausible vision for a "new Germany" beyond both fascism and Cold War machinations.

After the Communists dissolved the National Committee for a Free Germany (NKFD) in the weeks after the war, underground Nazi resistance groups began calling themselves the "Movement for a Free Germany." Lein argues that this circumstance was symbolic of the overall political trajectory at the time: "Other than the notable exceptions of Leipzig, Berlin and Munich, the antifascist movements described themselves as fighting organizations against fascism, and not as Committees for a Free Germany. Leaving the task of gathering social forces for "liberation" and thus, implicitly, renewing Germany to the Nazis and reactionaries characterized ... their defensive position."

Germans' failure to engage in popular resistance to Hitler even in the second half of the war understandably demoralized the Left and shook its faith in the masses' capabilities — a trait historian Martin Sabrowalso ascribes to the caste of Communist functionaries operating under Soviet tutelage in the East.

In the French, British, and American zones, Antifas began to recede by the late summer of 1945, marginalized by Allied bans on political organization and re-emerging divisions within the movement itself. The Social Democratic leadership under Kurt Schumacher sided with the Western occupiers and returned the party to its prewar anti-Communist line by the end of the year, decreeing that SPD membership was incompatible with participation in the Antifa movement.

In Stuttgart, the Antifa and what remained of the old trade union bureaucracy fought each other for political influence from the outset. The old leadership of the ADGB, prewar Germany's central trade union federation, sought to reestablish formalized employment relations in the occupied zones, which would at least mean a return to normalcy for Germany's working class. This ran counter to the approach of the Antifas, however, who cultivated strong ties to leftist shop stewards and factory committees, and usually called for nationalization and worker control of industry. These demands were ultimately not realistic in a shattered economy occupied by powerful foreign armies.

The prospect of stability and a degree of economic recovery under the SPD simply proved more appealing to workers forced to choose between that and the principled but harrowing struggle put forward by the Antifa.

Antifas were further hindered by the decision by the Allies, particularly the United States and Britain, to cooperate with what remained of the Nazi regime below its most executive levels. Antifas seeking to imprison local Nazi leaders or purge municipal bureaucracies were often stopped by occupying authorities who preferred to integrate functionaries of the old state into new, ostensibly democratic institutions.

This had less to do with any particular affinity between the Allies and ex-fascist functionaries so much as it served the practical interests of keeping German society running under exceedingly difficult conditions without ceding influence to the reemerging radical left. Outnumbered and outgunned by the occupying powers and outmaneuvered by the SPD, the Antifa's influence in the three western zones of occupation would evaporate in less than a year. West German society stabilized, the Cold War polarized the continent, and the political forces of old Germany in alliance with Social Democracy and the emerging Western bloc consolidated their hold over the country.

The KPD, for its part, initially took on waves of new members, as its prestige rose in light of the Soviet victory over Hitler and broad anticapitalist sentiment. The party soon rebuilt its industrial bases, and by 1946 controlled just as many shop floor committees in the heavily industrialized Ruhr Region as the SPD. In his classic study of the German labor movement, *Die deutsche Arbeiterbewegung*, German scholar Arno Klönne places its total membership in the three Western zones of occupation at three hundred thousand in 1947, and six hundred thousand in the East prior to the founding of the SED in 1946.

Following a brief period of participation in postwar provisional governments, however, the Allies sidelined the KPD, and the party soon returned to its ultra-leftist line. It sealed its political irrelevance in 1951 with the passage of "Thesis 37," a position paper on labor strategy riddled with anti–Social Democratic and anti-trade-union slurs. The motion, passed at the party conference, obligated all KPD members to obey party decisions above and against trade union directives if necessary. This move obliterated Communist support in the factories veritably overnight and relegated the party to society's fringes. It failed to re-enter parliament in the 1953 elections and was banned by the West German government outright in 1956.

Developments were markedly different in the Soviet zone, but ultimately ended in perhaps an even grimmer dead end: that of SED leader Walter Ulbricht's thoroughly Stalinized German Democratic Republic (GDR). An old-school Communist cadre from the party's early years, Ulbricht had survived twenty years of Stalinist purges and fascist repression to lead the "Ulbricht Group," a team of exiled KPD functionaries who now returned from Moscow to rebuild the country under Soviet occupation.

Though the Red Army generals certainly did not have a particularly democratic or egalitarian vision for East Germany in mind, they rejected cooperation with the old Nazi hierarchy for their own reasons and for a while permitted Antifas and related institutions to operate relatively freely. Eyewitness accounts from as late as 1947 report of factories in East Germany's prewar industrial centers like Halle (traditional Communist strongholds) where KPD-led works councils exerted a decisive influence over factory life, confident enough to conduct negotiations and argue with Soviet authorities in some instances.

In an interview with *Jacobin* to be published later this year, veteran KPO activist Theodor Bergmann tells of Heinrich Adam, prewar KPO member and mechanic at the Zeiss optics factory in Jena who joined the SED in hopes of realizing socialist unity. Heinrich was an active Antifa and trade unionist who organized protests against the Soviets' decision to take the Zeiss factory as war reparations (he suggested building a new factory in Russia instead). Adam was kicked out of the party for his independent views in 1952, although never persecuted, and lived out his days in Jena on a modest state pension for antifascist veterans.

In Dresden, a group of roughly eighty Communists, Social Democrats, and members of the left-social democratic Socialist Workers Party (SAP) formed a committee in May 1945 to surrender the city to the Red Army, citing broadcasts from the NKFD as inspiration. In cooperation with Soviet authorities, this group subsequently raided food and weapons stores from the

German Labor Front and other Nazi institutions, and organized a distribution system for the city's populace in the first postwar weeks.

Reports from Soviet officials and the Ulbricht Group describe rival antifascist groups, generally tolerated by the occupation, which beyond arming residents and organizing shooting practice also arrested local Nazis and opened soup kitchens for refugees from the eastern provinces. Internal communications reveal that leading Communists thought little of the Antifa, dismissed by Ulbricht as "the antifascist sects" in a communiqué to Georgi Dimitrov in mid-1945.

The Ulbricht Group's initial goal was to incorporate as many of these antifascists into the KPD as possible, and feared that repression would repel rather than attract them. Former Ulbricht Group member Wolfgang Leonhard would later claim in his memoirs, *Child of the Revolution*, that Ulbricht explained to fellow Communist functionaries: "It's quite clear—it's got to look democratic, but we must have everything in our control."

This period ended as the German Democratic Republic began to establish itself as a Soviet-style one-party state in the late 1940s, particularly after relatively free elections in 1946 delivered disappointing returns. Former KPO members and other oppositionists permitted to join after the war were investigated for past political crimes, purged, and often imprisoned. In the workplaces, the SED sought to rationalize production and thus neutralize the instances of factory control and democratic representation that had emerged.

The establishment of the Free German Trade Federation (FDGB) in 1946 marked the beginning of the SED's attempt to establish party control over the factories. These "unions" in fact organized East German workers in line with the interests of their practical bosses, the East German state, and sought to buy their loyalty through "socialist competition" schemes, piece work, and union-sponsored vacation packages.

However, the "free" unions could not afford to phase out competitive elections overnight. Antifa activists were often elected to FDGB shop floor committees in early the years, thus exercising continued influence in the workplace for a bit longer. Some were integrated into mid-level management, while others refused to betray their principles and stepped down or were removed for political reasons.

The public split between the Soviet Union and Tito's Yugoslavia in 1948 accelerated Stalinization in the Soviet occupation zone, and these limited spaces of self-organization were soon shut down entirely. Subsequently, the GDR's antifascist tradition would be diluted, distorted, and refashioned into an ahistorical national origins myth in which the citizens of East Germany were officially proclaimed the "victors of history," but where little space remained for the real and complicated history, not to mention ambivalent role of Stalinized Communism, behind it.

Dare to Dream

Following their collapse in late 1945 and early 1946, Antifas would disappear from the German political stage for nearly four decades. The modern Antifa with which most people associate the term has no practical historical connection to the movement from which it takes its name, but is instead a product of West Germany's squatter scene and autonomist movement in the 1980s—itself a unique outgrowth of 1968 considerably less oriented towards the industrial working class than its Italian counterpart. The first Antifas functioned as platforms to organize against far-right groups like the National Democratic Party (NPD) in an autonomist movement still numbering in the tens of thousands of active members and capable of occupying entire city blocks in some West German metropoles.

As the far right began to rebuild in the wake of German reunification, expressed in shocking mob attacks against asylum-seekers in several eastern provinces in the early 1990s, Antifa increasingly became a movement unto itself: a national network of dedicated antifascist groups organized into the "Antifaschistische Aktion/Bundesweite Organisation" (AA/BO).

In some ways, these groups were the inverse of their progenitors: rather than a broad alliance of socialists and progressives from separate, ideologically distinct currents, they were single-issue groups, expressly radical but vague and deeply heterogeneous in their specifics. Rather than a point of departure for young activists into a broader socialist and political left, Antifas outside of major cities are often the only political game in town, and function as a counter-cultural space with their own fashion styles, music scenes, and slang, rather than a component of a rooted mass movement within wider society.

After the AA/BO split in 2001, Antifas continued to work locally and regionally as dedicated networks of antifascists opposing far-right demonstrations and gatherings, though many also take up other left-wing issues and causes. What remains of the squats and infrastructure built up between the 1970s and 1990s continue to serve as important organizing and socializing spaces for the radical left, and "Antifa" as movement, trope, and general political outlook will no doubt continue to exist for quite some time—but it would appear that this iteration of antifascism has also exhausted its political repertoire.

The movement has shrunken continuously since the late 1990s, fragmented across ideological lines and unable to adjust its original autonomist strategies to shifting patterns of urbanization and the rise of right-populism. Its most promising products of late—the mass mobilizations against neo-Nazi marches in cities like Dresden, as well as the formation of a new, distinctively post-autonomist current in the form of the Interventionist Left—mark a departure from rather than a revival of classical Antifa strategy.

Antifascism has surged to the fore of debates on the American left under Trump's presidency, and many of the tactics and visual styles of the German Antifa can be seen emerging in cities like Berkeley and elsewhere. Some argue that with the arrival of European-style neo-fascist movements on American shores, it is also time to import European Antifa tactics in response.

Yet the Antifa of today is not a product of a political victory from which we can draw our own strength, but of defeat—

socialism's defeat at the hands of Nazism and resurgent global capitalism, and later the exhaustion of the autonomist movement in the wake of the neoliberal turn and the sweeping gentrification of many German cities.

Although Antifas continue to function as important poles of attraction for radicalizing youth and guarantee that the far right rarely goes unopposed in many European countries, its political form is of an exclusive nature, couched in its own aesthetic and rhetorical style and inaccessible to the masses of uninitiated people getting involved in activism for the first time. A left-wing subculture with its own social spaces and cultural life is not the same thing as a mass social movement, and we cannot afford to confuse the two.

Of course, the Antifa's experience in 1945 offers us equally few concrete lessons for how to fight a resurgent far right in the Trump era. Looking back at the history of the socialist left is not about distilling victorious formulas to be reproduced in the twenty-first century, but rather understanding how previous generations understood their own historical moment and built political organizations in response, in order to develop our own (hopefully more successfully models) for today.

The Antifas in Stuttgart, Braunschweig, and elsewhere faced impossible odds, but still sought to articulate a series of political demands and a practical organizational vision for the radicalizing workers willing to listen. Antifas refused to capitulate to their seemingly hopeless predicament and dared to dream big. Facing an even more fragmented and weakened left than in 1945, American antifascists will have to do the same.

Antifa Is Based on a Rejection of Fascism, but Its Factions Also Embrace Specific Positive Goals

Lisa Dunn

Lisa Dunn is a journalist based in Durham, North Carolina. She covers politics, reproductive rights, travel, stand-up comedy, literature, and more. She has written features, investigative news, book reviews, author interviews, travel tips, SEO content, and essays for GQ, Elite Daily, UPROXX, *and* Portland Monthly, *among others.*

After violence erupted at an Aug. 27 white supremacist rally in Berkeley, California, Antifa, a leftist movement, has, once again, been thrust into the spotlight. The violence that occurred has left many wondering what Antifa does. Are they dangerous? Aren't *they* the fascists?

Well, the question is simple and so, it turns out, is the answer.

The Basics

First things first: Antifa is short for "anti-fascist." And they are exactly what their name says. They say they oppose fascism "by any means necessary," according to Mark Bray, a historian and Antifa expert who wrote about them for *The Washington Post.*

To dig a little further: Antifa is a loosely organized collective of leftists with varying political beliefs. You can be a communist and Antifa. You can be a Democratic Socialist and Antifa. You can be an anarchist and Antifa.

Some cities have active chapters that hold regular meetings, but they're not so much a traditional organization as they are a political movement or ideology. Members come together for one main purpose: defeating fascism. In the United States, Antifa is

"What Does Antifa Do? The Movement Exists in Many Places," by Lisa Dunn, Elite Daily, August 31, 2017. Reprinted by permission.

also explicitly anti-racist, according to Bray. These groups are also more often than not anti-capitalist and anti-government.

A Brief History of the Movement

Their history is a bit muddy, but according to *The Economist*, Antifa grew from Anti-Fascist Action, an umbrella name for anti-fascism and anti-Nazism political movements in 1930s Europe. Anti-Fascist Action re-emerged at the end of World War II and organized alliances with socialists and communists to go after Nazis and organize politically.

They re-emerged yet again in the 1980s, as the skinhead and neo-Nazi movement grew in Europe, and simultaneously developed in the United States as Anti-Racist Action. In fact, Anti-Racist Action and Antifa are so closely related that Anti-Racist Action lists Antifa chapters as affiliates.

The Antifa movement re-emerges whenever neo-Nazi and fascist threats start to grow.

What Do They Want?

The short version is this: White supremacy is growing in the United States, according to a CBS News report, and Antifa believes that with white supremacy comes fascism.

After all, fascism, though hard to pin down exactly, stresses race and national identity, and it advocates total control of people and their identities, not individualism. That emphasis on white nationalism is at odds with the changing face of the United States, which is becoming less white, less Christian, and more heavily populated by immigrants.

In short? Antifa wants to prevent fascism and racism from rising in the United States.

What Does Antifa Do?

It depends on the chapter. Many Antifa chapters track local racist, neo-Nazi, and fascist activity, and they try to fight it at every chance. Rose City Antifa, the Portland, Oregon chapter, for instance, organizes direct actions, educational and solidarity events, and tries to creative leftist spaces. According to Rose City Antifa, their goal is to make sure fascism doesn't have a safe space to organize and grow.

One of their main functions is to show up at right-wing rallies and protests—like the Aug. 12 Unite the Right rally that led to anti-racist counter-protester Heather Heyer's death—to counteract messages of hate, racial purity, and fascism.

OK, But I've Heard That They're Violent

There are absolutely instances of violence from Antifa members. The violence that erupted in Berkeley over the weekend of August 25-27, for instance, was committed by Antifa individuals, dressed in black, according to *The Washington Post*.

Incidents like this are where the line "Antifa are the real fascists" comes from. After all, fascism and violence are closely related, as many fascists believed in achieving their goals by any means necessary.

But the nature of Antifa—a loose collective of leftist individuals—means that there will be outliers. Some will interpret their principle "by any means necessary" to mean violence. There will be individual instances of violence, from person to person, chapter to chapter. That doesn't make it OK, and the violence that occurred was condemned by many on the right and the left, including Rep. Nancy Pelosi. This, however, doesn't mean that Antifa as a whole should be condemned.

We should also keep in mind that there were also instances of Antifa protecting peaceful protesters from right-wing attacks at Charlottesville, according to first-hand accounts published by Slate.

So, at the end of the day, what is Antifa? A lot of things. But mostly, they're exactly what they proclaim themselves: Anti-Fascists.

Antifa's Decentralized Structure Contributes to the Movement's Ideological Diversity

Shawn McCreesh

Shawn McCreesh is a writer and editorial assistant at the New York Times. *His writing has appeared in* Rolling Stone, Men's Journal, *and the* Times.

I f you picked your jaw up off the floor just long enough to scratch your head and puzzle at what President Trump meant by the "alt-left" during his now infamous "Remarks on Infrastructure" meltdown on Tuesday, you're not alone.

"OK, what about the alt-left," he proffered, "what about the alt-left that came charging at the, as you say, the alt-right?"

So, what about the alt-left? Does it exist, or is it another bullet-dipped-in-pigs-blood fairy tale of Trump's imagination?

The word no doubt entered the president's consciousness the same way all his wildest policy ideas, hopes, dreams and paranoid delusions do—from tuning in to Fox.

Though it began as an insult within the left—a way to further deride the far left and so-called "Bernie Bros" during and after November's election—the right has adopted the phrase, as well. Sean Hannity and other, fringier monsters of the far-right media ecosystem have been, for at least a year now, pushing the idea of the "alt-left" as some sort of answer to the charge that the "alt-right," a very real political entity, has hijacked and poisoned the Republican party. *The Washington Post* best described it in 2016 as "The GOP's response: I know what you are but what am I."

But there is an actual active and growing group that Trump refers to. However, it's incorrect to name-check it as the alt-left and it's downright wrong to morally equivocate it with the neo-Nazi and white supremacist scum that stormed Charlottesville. But it does exist. Only it's called "antifa," short for anti-fascist, and it far predates Donald Trump.

First, a bit of history.

Anti-fascism originated in the years leading up to the second World War as a means to fight the spread of fascism across Europe, but in America the progenitors of what Trump would have you call the alt-left can be traced back to 1980s Minnesota. It was during this time that the group "Anti-Racist Action" sprung up around the Twin Cities to combat the rise of local Nazi skinheads. A.R.A., as the group became known, opened chapters across the US and won some major victories against neo-Nazis in the pre-Internet Eighties and Nineties.

Underground, local punk scenes often served as the stage for these groups to do battle, but the scale and frequency with which they clashed was enough to seep into the popular culture throughout the decade. It ultimately culminated with 1998's *American History X,* for which Edward Norton was nominated for an Academy Award for his performance as a reformed neo-Nazi skinhead.

These forerunners to what Trump and Hannity call the alt-left were so successful at banishing white supremacists back in to the shadows of society that, without a rallying cause, they dissipated in most places themselves.

"By the mid-2000s it started to peter out," says Mark Bray, a visiting historian of political radicalism at Dartmouth and author of *Antifa: The Anti-Fascist Handbook,* which comes out later this month. But now, thanks to white supremacists' newfound confidence to step out in to the public, the old A.R.A.-style groups have made a comeback, rebranded in the age of Trump.

"There's come another wave of folks who started to use the antifa name instead of Anti-Racist Action, and a lot of those groups started to get going in 2011, 2012 and 2013," says Bray. It was around this time that white supremacist Richard Spencer coined the term "alt-right." The rise of that movement served as an accelerant for the nascent antifa groups to expand into what Trump refers to today.

"As someone who pays attention to what goes on with the far left in the US, [anti-facism has become] a focal point for politics that was not on the radar back when Occupy Wall Street was going on," he says. "There were groups, but it wasn't a focus on the left."

There are hundreds, likely thousands of active anti-fascists (or, "antifas," as they are called) across the country, although it's hard to pin down an exact number because their movement is so fragmentary and purposely decentralized. There is no Richard Spencer or Milo Yiannopolous equivalent within their movement and anonymity is perhaps their central tenet. Antifas organize in hyper-local crews of eight to 12, which they call "affinity groups," as a way to protect against being infiltrated. New York, Atlanta, Portland, Oregon and Philly are known to be particularly active hubs.

This modern incarnation of anti-fascism had become infamous earlier this year—long before Trump's Tuesday shout-out—primarily for its use of the "black bloc" tactic, wherein multiple "affinity groups," dressed head-to-toe in black converge upon a public demonstration where white supremacists are known to be. Black blocs exist to cause mayhem and are known to leave a trail of destruction—and sometimes violence—in their wake.

This destructive streak—coupled with disregard for neo-Nazis' right to free speech—has not endeared these groups to the Democratic party in the way that much of the GOP has welcomed the so-called alt-right.

"They are illiberal," says Bray. "They don't believe in society as a value neutral public sphere where any kind of ideas can just float around."

It's this philosophy that justifies the chaos they're capable of causing, perhaps most evidently on display the day of Trump's inauguration in Washington DC, when a black bloc materialized to wreck businesses, torch a limo and punch Richard Spencer in the face, giving us the hit heard 'round the Internet. Similar spats have since occurred wherever so-called alt-right figures like Yiannopolous or Spencer try to promote their hate-speech publicly. Berkeley has been one such frequented battleground, but showdowns in places such as Charlottesville and, before that, Pikeville, Kentucky, prove that these groups—on both the left and right—and their radical ideas exist and operate not just in the youthful and idealistic petri-dishes of liberal-arts school campuses, but in towns and cities across the country.

Anti-fascists view the events that transpired in Virginia last week and the president's subsequent remarks as a watershed moment in the fight against their seemingly ever-ascendant ideological nemesis. "On our side, it's war," says one anti-fascist group leader who was present at Charlottesville and has participated in black bloc activity in cities up and down the East Coast since Trump's election. "Expect greater support from average people. A lot of [normal people] and libs who would have told us to f*ck off and stop being so upsetting are now crossing over into our side. We are seeing a new wave of membership coming in."

Their ranks had already been swelling pre-Charlottesville, too. An anti-fascist who goes by James Anderson—and is the administrator of the website It's Going Down, which serves as both the chief news outlet and a digital town hall for antifa—told me in an interview last spring that the rise in far right violence seen under Trump "has forced a lot of people on the left to actually look at anti-fascism and take it seriously."

"This sh*t is real, it's touching people's lives, and there's a very clear line being drawn by the Trump administration that it's acceptable, permitted and part of the program," he said at the time. And that was five months *before* Trump's near-endorsement of neo-Nazi riffraff from his bigot pulpit this week.

The Political Network Known as Antifa Is Organized Around Reactionary Ideals, but That Is Not the End of the Story

Whitney Mallett

Whitney Mallett is a video producer and freelance journalist whose writing has been featured in VICE, Pin-Up Magazine, *and* Interview Magazine. *Her work focuses on the intersection between art, piracy, politics, and criminal justice.*

On the first Saturday of March, just blocks from the Berkeley campus of the University of California, an ultra-nationalistic rally met anti-fascist resistance. It was one of several pro-Trump assemblies around the country that day, and while some in the crowd sported MAKE AMERICA GREAT AGAIN hats and homemade signs arguing against political correctness, some of the 100 or so Trump supporters brandished gas masks on their faces and knives on their waistbands.

By 2 PM, there was a crowd of equal or greater size gathered for a counter-demonstration. A young woman with a nose ring carried a RESIST TRUMP sign. Two others, both in dark jeans, hoodies, and bandannas hiding half their faces, held a banner that read ANTI-FASCIST ZONE with three arrows, angled down and to the left, drawn inside the O as a nod to the 1930s anti-Nazi organization the Iron Front. In fact, a sizable portion of the anti-Trump crowd was masked and dressed in black—a sartorial cohesion that read as intimidating but was first and `foremost an effort to keep the wearers anonymous, shielded from law enforcement and alt-right doxing.

These demonstrators belonged to the Antifa (short for anti-fascism) movement and clashed with Trump supporters in the middle of the park's green lawn that day. The skirmish started

"California Anti-Fascists Want Racists and the Trump Administration to Be Afraid," by Whitney Mallett, Vice Media LLC, May 9, 2017. Reprinted by permission.

with shouting matches and quickly escalated to brawls marked by punches and pepper spray. Within a couple hours, knives had allegedly been drawn, blood had been spilled, and ten arrests had been made. Small bonfires made up of MAKE AMERICA GREAT AGAIN hats and American flags littered the lawn. By 5:30 PM, there were still a dozen counter-demonstrators yelling at the dregs of the Trump rally still remaining. "When was America ever great?" a black man with a bit of gray in his hair asked, demanding a response from the last supporter wearing a red cap. But the Trump supporter walked away, never offering an answer.

That same day, bandanna-clad Antifa members protested pro-Trump rallies across the country, but only a few of these demonstrations turned violent. Berkeley's clash resulted in more arrests than any of the other rallies nationwide, and it marked the third time since last summer that Bay Area Antifa conflicts have made the news. In the wake of the election, the tension felt across the country has a different tenor in the Bay Area, in part because the region has a long history of anarchist organizing dating back to the turn of the 20th century. Following Trump's victory last November, 7,000 people took to the streets in Oakland with protests lasting for three nights: They lit garbage cans on fire. They threw bricks through car-dealership windows. Thirty of them were arrested.

During the fracas at the rally in March, one of the Antifa demonstrators explained to me the thinking behind their protest. "The point of it is not to give them a platform. You don't give fascism a platform because once you give it a platform, it becomes normalized," Devin Lawson* said. He went on to address the violence that had erupted, adding: "Sometimes you have to use direct action to stop it because protesting, signs, yelling is not going to do anything. You have to make them afraid."

There's a grassroots punk quality to the way Antifa mobilize underground. And it's likely that anti-Trump protesters heard about the gathering the same way I did: Through a hotline, you can call for details on music shows at DIY venues and protests coming up in San Francisco, Oakland, and Berkeley. The anarchist-news site Itsgoingdown.org helped facilitate counter-demonstrations by listing the locations and times of all the pro-Trump rallies happening on March 4. Some activists have built peer-to-peer networks as well, passing information between one another via encrypted-texting services like Signal.

The clash in March followed an analogous situation just a month before, during which a similarly outfitted mob of masked protesters shut down Milo Yiannopoulos's appearance at the Berkeley campus. Yiannopoulos, at the time still yet to be exiled from alt-right circles for his comments on pedophilia, had been invited by the Berkeley College Republicans, but following an article published on Breitbart.com about his campaign against sanctuary campuses, some opponents believed that he intended to out undocumented students during his speech. Networks of anti-fascist organizers mobilized a group of students and nonstudents alike to forcefully deny Yiannopoulos a platform to speak. There was a highly publicized clash between protesters and the police, the talk was canceled, and for days many media outlets sensationalized the skirmish and argued for or against Yiannopoulos's right to free speech. But to those who participated in the protest, it was a clear victory.

"It was kind of amazing," Jade, an 18-year-old Antifa newbie, told me. "There were drums and people yelling, chanting into megaphones. Then the crowd parts, and you see this swarm of dudes dressed in black with flags. They ripped away the barricades, tipped over that generator, and the rest is history." The protest against Yiannopoulos was the first action she participated in. She was at the Trump counter-demonstration, too. "I'm a queer Jewish trans woman," she explained. "I have a personal interest in anti-fascism as far as my different intersectionalities."

Jade didn't know anything about Antifa when she arrived in the Bay Area less than a year ago. "I just moved here to get away from my parents," she told me. The string of police shootings of black men that occurred over the past several years encouraged her to become involved with Antifa anarchists. Once she did, she said, she also found a family in the movement.

Antifa's roots go back to the early 1930s and the *Antifaschistische* movement that organized to oppose the rise of Nazism in Germany. The movement was rekindled in the 1980s as skinhead culture rose in popularity and far-right leaders took office throughout the US and Western Europe. Stateside, Anti-Racist Action (ARA) was formed in 1987. "It was a group of anti-racist skinhead punks who got together and created ARA," Alexander Reid Ross, author of *Against the Fascist Creep* and adjunct professor at Portland State University, told me. In America, decentralized networks of activists devoted to fighting fascism and racism have adopted the Antifa nomenclature during the last decade. "It was through Rose City Antifa," Ross said, referring to a Portland group that grew out of the ARA, "that the European and American models were sort of synthesized and the current model of Antifa in the US was developed."

Taking cues from similar European organizations, American Antifa groups often use "black bloc" tactics, but while that term is sometimes used as interchangeable with "Antifa," they mean very different things. Black bloc, Ross explained, is "the mobilization of a group wearing black clothing and black bandannas with black hoods or hats to maintain anonymity in the context of some kind of protest." In the US, he said, Antifa "is an anonymous framework for an organization that gathers intelligence on local fascist groups and either publishes that information for the public, sends that information to other groups who have a vested interest in shutting those groups down, or openly confronts those groups, whether it's through direct action or calling for a civil-society protest. The two things are absolutely not synonymous. In fact, black bloc tactics have been used by fascists."

As leftists and liberals come together against the Trump administration, there's some division over the use of black bloc tactics. At an International Women's Day rally in San Francisco, just a few days after the violent clashes at the Trump rally, black-bandannaed youth were visible alongside women in pussy hats. Jade, masked in all black, endured some heckling. A man jeered,

"Don't break anything. I don't want to get arrested because of you." Sarah, one of the rally's organizers, addressed the palpable divisions in the crowd. "Some people are masked up. That is a tactic of safety, so stand in solidarity with them," she urged into a microphone. A middle-aged blond woman challenged her, demanding, "Why are you supporting black bloc?"

The argument frequently made against violence and property destruction is that it makes the larger fight—the opposition to the Trump administration—look bad. Of the clash at the anti-Trump protest in March, Katharine Harer, a woman at the Women's Day rally, said, "I don't think it helps our cause right now. I think maybe we'll reach a point where we will have to be really militant in a more forceful way, but I think right now the best thing to do is to congregate in large groups to pressure our legislators." A Change.org petition that has almost met its signatory goal is calling for President Trump to declare Antifa a domestic terrorist organization, asserting that terrorism is "the use of intentionally indiscriminate violence as a means to create terror or fear, in order to achieve a political, religious, or ideological aim," and that the movement fits this criteria. Others I talked to at the Women's Day rally, including an attendee named Imri Rivas, suggested shifting the focus from debating violence to how direct actions can be used to build collective autonomy between communities.

Throughout the Bay Area, there are many organizations, which overlap with and exist within the same ecosystem as Antifa, committed to building these kinds of autonomous communities through urban-farming projects, radical hacker collectives, anarchist presses, and anti-capitalist art making. Street fights and property destruction, however, make the news more often than these other activities. While it may be frustrating that the use of violence overshadows other community-building efforts, resistance to violence as a tactic, Ross argues, ignores the realities of political struggle. "Violent opposition to fascism is the way that anti-fascists have organized for decades and decades. A lot of people come to anti-fascist organizing thinking, *This is going to be like Occupy. The* worst that could happen is that somebody could break a window. But that is just not the reality," he said. "This is the reality of political struggle that white people have been sheltered from. Other people have to deal with racist violence all the time. There's a real question of how those communities can defend themselves and how we can support those communities defending themselves."

Anarchists see transformative potential in disobeying the state's rules about what is and isn't appropriate behavior. Their goal is to "make the situation get out of the control of the police and put the people in the street in power," James Anderson, from Itsgoingdown.org, explained to me. "Psychologically, when, at a protest, people start to spray graffiti or they break a bank window or a brick goes through a cop car, it sets off the understanding that there's a different mode of activity that's happening. A wide range of human actions can suddenly be possible."

In 2014, when it was announced that Officer Darren Wilson would not be indicted for the murder of Michael Brown, there were riots in Oakland that lasted for 17 days. Highways were blockaded. Cop cars were vandalized. Garbage cans were lit on fire. Anderson suggested a reason, beyond the goal of reclaiming power, for why these actions have become popular: "This sh*t is fun. This is what young people want to do. They want to engage in a political project that includes them, includes their friends, and actually puts agency into what they are doing. It's not just this stale symbolic gesture." But the method can be dangerous for both sides. During the skirmish at the pro-Trump rally, Antifa activists were bloodied, and last June, during a confrontation between Sacramento anti-fascists and a neo-Nazi group, ten people were wounded. Still, the most dedicated members of the movement maintain that in order to prevent the rise of fascist sentiments, violence is necessary.

The brand of right-wing extremism that American Antifa groups have traditionally mobilized against is on the rise. According to the Southern Poverty Law Center, "in the last two years, in part due to a presidential campaign that flirted heavily with extremist ideas, the hate group count has risen again." And Bay Area organizers are committed to countering this mainstreaming of hate. The weekend following the International Women's Day rally, a two-day conference called the Revolutionary Organizing Against Racism, brought together local and visiting anti-fascist and anti-racist organizers. The next week, a couple dozen anti-fascists and anarchists rallied outside a Berkeley BART train station in black bloc uniform with banners and flyers warning against nationalist attacks. They say the action strove to drum up more support for a counter-demonstration at an April 15 Freedom rally.

Right-wing extremism is glomming onto the Trump administration and gaining momentum, and anti-fascist frontline fighters do not appear to be slowing down as their ranks are bolstered by anti-Trump sentiment. For now, the two parties clash head-on in real time, and it remains difficult to know how meaningful these conflicts might turn out to be.

Antifa's Posture of Resistance Is Deliberate and Part of Its Effectiveness

Christopher Joseph

Christopher Joseph is a poet and political writer and activist from Providence, Rhode Island.

On February 1, 2017, Milo Yiannopoulos, alt-right speaker, provocateur, and Breitbart editor known for his conservative, misogynistic, and Islamophobic views was scheduled to speak at the UC Berkeley campus. Approximately 1,500 faculty and students assembled peacefully in protest, but a minority of protestors clothed in black and wearing black masks stormed the police barricades and shot fireworks at a campus building. A police spotlight was toppled and set aflame. Protests signs and banners read "THIS IS WAR" and "BECOME UNGOVERNABLE." The Black Bloc had arrived and caused a disruption that, to a casual observer on either side of the political aisle, presents as ungovernable chaos, and the event was canceled due to security concerns.

In this case, the Black Bloc protestors, known as anti-fascists or Antifa, achieved their goal. They are the radical leftists on our political spectrum, and they shut down Yiannopoulos' lecture and, in doing so, destroyed a platform for the offensive views that he promotes—views that anti-fascist activists have directly and physically confronted since pre-World War II Europe. To destroy a platform or forum for fascistic speech and assembly is historically a core objective of Antifa, and the Black Bloc, which is a unified group of protestors dressed head to toe in black and wearing masks to avoid identification, has long been a favored organizational tactic of anti-fascists, so while this may appear new and radical to some, it does have quite a bit of successful history behind it. Anti-fascists were partly responsible for the downfall of Mussolini, and Black Bloc marches have confronted and ousted Neo-Nazi gangs. However, at the heart of their objectives lie two important questions. First, doesn't Yiannopoulos (or any other similar speaker) also have first amendment rights, which were ultimately denied? Second, why choose violence, intimidation, or property damage as a protest tactic?

Truthfully, neither of the above lines of questioning will result in a concrete, definitive "yes or no" answer or "right or wrong" choice. It is a debate that cannot be won, and at this point in the argument, we are subject to our ideologies and semblances of conscience, as well as our personal preferences for political expression and action. However, understanding exactly what happened at UC Berkeley is important to understanding protest—the vocal and physical manifestation of the first amendment—in the contemporary United States, and especially under the Trump administration.

Today, the nation is politically polarized to the extent that those in opposing camps almost categorically refuse to listen to one another. George Saunders termed this dichotomy as "LeftLand and RightLand" in his essay on Trump supporters in the *New Yorker*, and today we can even see such ideological dismissal in the Senate, when Senator Elizabeth Warren was ordered by Majority Leader Mitch McConnell to stop reading aloud, on the Senate floor in official proceedings, a letter written by Coretta Scott King in 1986 regarding Senator Jeff Sessions' racist views and actions. King was attempting to persuade the Senate to deny Sessions a federal judgeship, and she succeeded. Warren read the letter as evidence that Sessions is unfit to serve as the United States Attorney General under Trump. McConnell didn't want to hear it and claimed that Warren "impugned" Sessions, so he shut down her platform using an arcane procedural rule and dismissed her views as unwelcome.

It's safe to say that neither side really wants to hear from the other and that we tend to surround ourselves with people of like-minded ideologies. When we do hear from the other side, tempers on both sides tend to flare. Of course, there are people who reject that notion and purposefully seek to understand those with opposing views, to show them empathy, and to perhaps attempt to convince them that they are wrong in a civil, respectful, and lawful manner, with hope for positive change. But to do so requires a belief in civility and respect from both parties—essentially, a fundamental belief in the right of the other to exist peacefully and without threat—and when one party preaches, for example, a hatred of members of a specific religion or race or nationality or gender (especially when coupled with a violent call to action in the manner of the KKK or Nazi Germany), then all civility is already lost and there is no dialogue to be had. To preach, for example, Islamophobic or misogynistic views is, by its oppressive and intolerant nature, not a civil act. It is an offensive act, and offensive acts warrant certain forms of response.

That is not an argument against the freedom to speak such offensive views—Antifa also believes in second chances for known racists, fascists, white supremacists, etc., if they are willing to change—but rather an argument in favor of direct action against oppressive speech. As I've written before, first amendment rights are universal, but so is the right to respond to speech that offends and causes people to feel violated or unsafe because of their identity. Such a response is an act of defense. The legality of any response is only protected so far as the first amendment goes, meaning that illegal responses such as violence, property damage, etc. are not within one's rights even if they are within one's morals and capabilities. That being said, Yiannopoulos is free to give a lecture and say mostly whatever he wants, short of abject hate speech, which is as criminal as violence is, and people are free to loudly disagree with him en masse.

Many UC Berkeley students and faculty chose the path of loud, en masse, yet peaceful and nonviolent opposition in the form of protest. Antifa went a step further by seeking to extinguish any sort of hateful, divisive, oppressive, or fascistic speech at the very source. At UC Berkeley, they chose disruptive and arguably violent tactics such as fireworks, property damage, and the destruction of police barricades that created enough of a security disruption at the venue so that Yiannopoulos was unable to speak. Therefore, it isn't that his rights were denied, but rather that an environment was created wherein it would be dangerous and foolish, if not impossible, for him to preach hatred or division. As such, Yiannopoulos' platform was destroyed.

To "destroy the platform" is a textbook anti-fascist tactic that organizations have used for decades, historically in efforts to break up Neo-Nazi gangs and other fascistic organizations and to prevent their return, and is currently in use against members of the alt-right. The rowdy protest outside of the DeploraBall on the inaugural eve, complete with black masks and flaming trash cans, is such an example. Essentially, anti-fascism declares that any attempt to gain a platform to espouse fascistic or oppressive views or to organize action around such ideologies (i.e. Yiannopoulous's Islamophobia or Richard Spencer's anti-Semitism), is an inherently uncivil and offensive act and will be met with immediate physical resistance. That declaration relies on the aforementioned understanding that civility is automatically lost when any form of fascism is brought into the discourse, and especially into the public sphere of influential speech, because fascism itself historically speaks the language of violence by advocating for xenophobia, militant nationalism, racial superiority, war, and ethnic cleansing and genocide.

A simplistic but incorrect way to explain this conflict of ideologies in the form of physical resistance is to say that Antifa is "fighting fire with fire." However, when an Antifa group destroys a platform, they're not fighting with fire. Instead, they're putting the metaphorical fire out by eliminating any chance for a fascistic group to assemble and for their views to be publicly spoken and disseminated, which is based on the presumption that such assemblies provide an exchange of ideas that can foment bigoted or discriminatory views and, in the worst of cases, inspire or incite racially motivated violence. In the case of UC Berkeley, smashed windows and fireworks destroyed the platform. Many on both sides of the aisle will argue that such tactics "look bad" and are dangerous, immoral, intolerant, or illegal, or may cause the opposing camp to unify and respond even more aggressively. Amid cries on both sides for peaceful and lawful protest (if any protest at all), Antifa will be denounced for their violent actions without any regard to the fact that they exist to prevent further violence in the form of fascist speech and action, in which case their use of "violence" is largely defensive (they are also known to defend Jewish neighborhoods). The media will frame such confrontations to polarize views on the matter without offering any critical insight as to why certain protestors choose such tactics. But anti-fascist protestors must know the legal consequences of their actions, as well as the subsequent visibility (hence the black mask), and they most likely weighed the moral implications of their decisions long before they smashed windows and launched fireworks. After all, these are strategic, targeted choices stemming from an unequivocal political and moral imperative.

Many everyday Americans who are not anti-fascists and who may have never heard the term will protest on the streets, on the highways, in the airports, and on state and federal property in the coming months and years as we face a fascistic Trump administration that is under the guidance Steven Bannon, an executive of Breitbart News and a known white supremacist, which stands as proof that American white supremacy can gain the highest platform and the most power possible. Millions have already protested with many small victories to show for their efforts. The vast majority will likely continue to do so peacefully and nonviolently, yet Republicans across the country have dubbed protests as "economic terrorism" and are already attempting to enact legislation that would outlaw effective nonviolent forms of protest, such as blocking an interstate or wearing a mask, and some laws even seek to legalize vehicular manslaughter in such instances. (And this meme shows that at least some Trump supporters on the internet like that idea.) The J20 inauguration disruptors who faced tear gas and pepper spray are up against unprecedented felony riot charges that carry a 10 year prison sentence when, other than the isolated incident of Richard Spencer getting punched on camera, no protestors committed violent acts against actual people—just trash cans, bank windows, and a limousine, with some graffiti to boot. That is better termed as targeted property damage or vandalism, not violence. Black Lives Matter, a nonviolent movement against police brutality and for racial justice, was met with riot police in Ferguson and faced the same aggressive police tactics. The Standing Rock Sioux Water Protectors have faced constant violent incursions for protesting the Dakota Access Pipeline, and militant police tear-gassed, pepper-sprayed, lobbed concussion grenades, blasted cold water in sub-freezing temperatures, and shot rubber bullets at unarmed and peaceful protestors, resulting in severe injuries.

Considering all of these events and their individual actors, what are the specifically violent acts that resulted in human pain, injury, and suffering versus some form of nonviolent disruption? Who is actually to blame for such violence, and who is committing it or inciting it? Who is allowed to use such violence, and when, and why, and against who? Despite legality, what is the moral cause for nearly blowing a young protestor's arm off with a concussion grenade, or for tear gassing a Black Bloc, or for shooting and killing unarmed, innocent black men? These are questions that we must continue to ask ourselves in a nation that is growing increasingly intolerant to protest and civil disobedience, in a state apparatus that deploys a highly militarized police force that has a history of racial discrimination, and in a time when protest in all forms is imperative to defending civil liberties and human rights, it becomes necessary to choose the method that suits your beliefs and has the greatest chance to advance your cause and achieve any and all possible victories.

For some, a victory is to remain nonviolent and pressure their elected officials to resist or enact a specific policy, or to raise awareness for a cause and build organizational structure. That is an admirable and necessary objective. For others, a victory is to destroy a fascistic platform and stop hate speech before it starts. That is also an admirable and necessary objective. Right now, in

Trump's America, any protest that disrupts a fascistic event or policy, defends our rights and the rights of those less privileged, seeks to challenge power and authority and the state use of violence, or acts as a vehicle for grassroots organization is not only a welcome opportunity for citizens to become aware and involved, but is becoming a vital civic duty that demands the involvement of all who are able and willing. Most importantly, any protest that can attempt to defuse the tensions between LeftLand and RightLand by seeking common ground, no matter how unlikely, will certainly be heralded as a civic achievement of our times.

For those of us in the fight and for those to come, remember that any manner of protest is a personal choice dictated by an individual's circumstances and beliefs. We all protest for our own reasons and we should respect each individual's choices, even if we disagree. For Antifas, they are there in solidarity to target and destroy all acts of fascism, even if fireworks and smashed windows are necessary, in defense of human rights and dignity. Such tactics, while radical, disruptive, and arguably violent, succeed in intimidating and ousting those who seek to vocalize and enact discrimination, hatred, and violence against innocent and oppressed people. Those who use such tactics are unconcerned with the free speech rights of those they oppose; they know that their opponents do not fundamentally believe in tolerance or respect for all humanity, and so they offer them none in return. It is arguably a militant stance to take, but in the case of UC Berkeley and Milo Yiannopoulos, it is an effective course of action.

Antifa Lacks a Distinct Positive Political Vision

Vasin Douglas

Vasin Douglas is a writer and media management expert. He is currently Operation Manager at CNN *Digital.*

U nlike other groups which lean to the far left or the far right —or organisations classified as hate groups—Antifa does not advocate any particular doctrine.

The rise of President Donald J. Trump has emboldened a number of right-wing groups, Antifa has presented itself as a counter to this rise in right-wing activity.

In August 2017, when President Trump used the term "Antifa" to denounce a group of demonstrators in Charlottesville, Virginia, he brought renewed attention to the roiling racial divisiveness which has characterized this past US presidential election. However, most observers of the news may not have heard of the disparate groups which form Antifa until recent months. Now its motives and membership are under scrutiny after it has physically resisted neo-Nazis, the Ku Klux Klan (KKK), white nationalist, the alt-right and white supremacists during rallies and protests.

In simple terms, Antifa is a self-styled antifascist group. The ultimate goal of its members is to oppose and fight fascism through protest and direct confrontation. Since the election of Donald Trump, there has been a rise in right-wing extremist activity. In response, Antifa has increased its activity. Through use of Twitter, Facebook, websites, word of mouth, fliers and graffiti, Antifa is unifying independent groups to oppose far-right organizations. Antifa even has a step-by-step guide to organizing your own local Antifa group.

"The Origins and Aims of Antifa—The Face of Anti-fascism in America," by Vasin Douglas, WikiTribune, October 12, 2017. https://www.wikitribune.com/story/2017/10/12/politics/analysis-the-origins-and-aims-of-antifa/4265/. Licensed under CC BY-SA 3.0 Unported.

The history of Antifa is older and more complex than it appears. One theory suggests that the name may have its origins in the Antifaschistische Aktion movement, which started in opposition to fascist movements in Italy and Germany in the early 20th century. According to Mark Bray, author of *The Anti-fascist Handbook*, during the 1980s, US anti-fascists took on the name Anti-Racist Action Network. The name fell out of favor during the 2000s. The current wave of antifascists have taken on the name and image of the post World War II European Antifa.

Autonomous Local Action

Antifa is now shorthand for anti-fascist or anti-fascist action. The movement is known for using physical confrontation in order to achieve their goal of fighting fascism. Without official leadership, Antifa uses a network of autonomous local groups for its structure and strategically uses social media and the internet for communication.

Although critics have tried to find parallels between Antifa and traditional hate-groups like the KKK and neo nazis, there is little common ground.

To apply some context, the KKK is a terrorist organization that originated after the US Civil War. It is one of America's oldest hate groups, and a vigilante group established to intimidate Southern African-Americans through cross burnings, lynchings and murders. The goal of the KKK is to strip African-Americans of their civil rights, voting rights and economic rights.

Unlike other groups which lean to the far left or the far right, Antifa does not advocate a singular central doctrine. The lack of a central doctrine also means the Antifa movement is driven by a wide range of political motives, including anti-capitalism, environmentalism and gay rights. In recent years in the US, Antifa groups have allied themselves with members of the Black Lives Matter movement and other social-justice organizations.

This distinguishes them from other American entities like the KKK, which advocates racial purity. It also differentiates them from political parties such as the Nazis in Germany, who used genocide as a means of achieving their goals.

In the US, Antifa is not classified as a hate group by the Anti-Defamation League—which defines a hate group as an organization whose goals are based on a shared hatred towards different races, religions, ethnicities, nationalities, national origins, genders, and/or sexual identities. To be classified as a hate-group, the organization itself must have a hate-based purpose.

Antifa members usually gravitate towards a commonly shared ideological view which does not look to governments to solve a problem. More radical elements argue only violence can quell the rise of racism and fascism. Antifa groups also express disdain for mainstream liberal politics and the traditional media, which they view as protecting white supremacy and not working to support the oppressed. They specifically call out the American Civil Liberties Union (ACLU) and the Anti-Defamation League (ADL) as being inadequate and ill-prepared to fight against fascism—stating that their "middle of the road" position is the means by which racists and fascists have become legitimized.

Punching Spencer

One of the most vivid examples of how Antifa members differ from other traditional protest movements occurred last January during the inauguration of President Trump, when a masked Antifa member punched Richard B. Spencer—a prominent white supremacist—in the face. In September another noteworthy attack occurred in Seattle, Washington, when Antifa members used social media to track down a Nazi for harassing a black bus rider. Once they found him they physically attacked him and knocked him unconscious. These actions are a shock to a country with a long history of peace-abiding left-wing movements. What followed was a national debate over whether it was ever morally justifiable to "punch a Nazi."

Critics of Antifa say the movement ultimately opposes free speech. They argue white-supremacists like the KKK, neo-Nazis, alt-right groups and other white-nationalist organizations should be permitted to assemble in public without fear of resistance. They have also, according to *The Atlantic*, criticized the violent attacks by some members as alienating to sections of American society. They argue Antifa-related violence could contribute to the re-election of Trump in 2020.

Unlike members of the KKK, Antifa followers do not wear a uniform, but occasionally adopt clothing which helps avoid identification by the authorities. This may include black clothing, and masks or balaclavas. The face covering is employed to obscure a person's identity and, in some instances, intimidate opponents. This can be traced back to the anarchist movements of the "black bloc" coalition of the 1980s, who regularly wore similar attire to avoid prosecution.

As the political and social climate continues to polarize, there is one thing that the right and the left can agree on: they are not in favor of Antifa. Liberals such as US House minority leader Nancy Pelosi have condemned violent acts from Antifa demonstrations. Noam Chomsky criticized Antifa as being counterproductive, while right-wing extremists criticize Antifa for interfering with their 1st Amendment rights. What looks to be inevitable is that the US will see an increase in Antifa's protests as Nazi, KKK, White Nationalist and Alt-Right groups increase their activity.

In Order to Remain Relevant, Antifa Needs to Settle on a Clear Set of Political Goals

Dhruv Devulapalli

Dhruv Devulapalli is a researcher at the Whaley Group and writer for the California section of the Berkeley Political Review.

They showed up wearing black clothes and masks, throwing fireworks and smashing glass windows. They threatened people recording them, and attacked those who stood in their way. They set fires and threw Molotov Cocktails. Later, they were described as "Ninja-like" individuals who used "paramilitary tactics." But this wasn't a civil war or a terror attack. This was Antifa, a growing movement whose stated goal is to smash fascism.

Antifa groups have gained notoriety in recent years due to violent incidents around the country. In June 2016, Antifa Sacramento and other leftist organizations clashed with white nationalist groups. At the time, the far right Traditionalist Workers Party was organizing a rally outside the California State Capitol to "protest globalization" and "assert their free expression." In response, Antifa Sacramento issued statements on its website calling for direct action against these "Nazis." As the rally began, members of both sides arrived with masks and weapons. The groups attacked each other with sticks and knives, and a riot ensued. Ten people were hospitalized with cuts and stab wounds, and streets were shut down after what was described as "free-for-all violence" between the far-left and far-right.

Similar incidents occurred in the lead-up to the inauguration of Donald Trump, with Antifa groups rioting the day before a Women's March attended by thousands. More recently, in February 2017, Bay Area Antifa groups protested an event involving Milo Yiannopoulos, a right-wing blogger for Breitbart. Critics of

"Antifa: A New Political Resistance?" by Dhruv Devulapalli, Berkeley Political Review, March 23, 2017. Reprinted by permission.

Yiannopoulos have described him as a troll and a provocateur. Yiannopoulos was invited to speak at UC Berkeley by the Berkeley College Republicans. The event was scheduled to take place amidst intense student opposition, and over a thousand people attended what was intended to be a peaceful protest. The protest was interrupted by highly organized Antifa groups, which smashed windows, shot fireworks, and strategically set fires. The Antifa groups then started a riot which spread from the Berkeley campus to the streets downtown, where the groups damaged ATMs and looted a Starbucks ...

Despite its recent surge in notoriety, Antifa is not a new movement—it has its roots in political groups from the 1930s in Europe. These groups were primarily organized by communists and socialist democrats, and actively fought against Nazism and fascism during and after World War II. In the United States, the current movement began in the 1980s. One group belonging to the movement, Anti-Racist Action Network (ARA), originated to fight neo-Nazis in Minneapolis. Chapters soon rose across the country, where they violently clashed with neo-Nazis and skinheads on the streets and in the underground music scene, and organized protests against the KKK and other far-right organizations. These groups continued their political activism into the 2000s, protesting against the Iraq War. Over the past decade, Antifa groups in California have risen to prominence. Protesters today use "black bloc" tactics, which provide anonymity to violent activists. They use encryption to communicate, although a large part of their organization is online, and many groups have their own websites. Black bloc protesters wear black clothing, scarves, sunglasses, ski masks, motorcycle helmets with padding, or other face-concealing and face-protecting items. Some of the tactics used by the group borrow from civil disobedience movements, including sit-ins, blockades, and disruptions. While the movement itself is de-centralized, Antifa groups in the Bay Area and Southern California share the common goal of "smashing fascism" with groups from across the country, such as NYC Antifa.

Despite the intense media scrutiny in the aftermath of recent events, the broader political motives of Antifa groups in the United States are still not widely known. The stated objective of most Antifa groups is to oppose fascism in all forms. However, the decentralization of the movement has meant that ideology and methods of protest are not uniform. US Antifa groups have adopted the "no platform" policies of their European counterparts, whereby they do not take a broad political stance in order to unify anti-fascist activists who may not agree on all political issues. As a result, the Antifa movement has many different, generally leftist, factions: communists, socialist democrats, and anarchists. The diverse motivations of different members of the movement has divided opinions on the left while enraging the right. Conservatives criticize the movement for its anarchist activities that violate the law and appear to stand against the Constitution and government in any form. Within the left, the group is criticized for being too radical, and for taking extra-legal measures to promote progressive policies. Since the group itself doesn't have a platform, it's unclear what its various factions will do in the future, or what their objectives will be after its goals are met. Will the group enter the mainstream once the political scenario is more conducive to their policies, or will the anarchist factions take over and continue to oppose any government?

As political opposition to the current administration grows, and grassroots involvement in liberal politics increases, Antifa groups will become more and more relevant. However, the groups will struggle to receive mainstream support due to their violent approach to activism. Conservatives have called for Antifa to be labelled a terrorist organization, while liberals are still divided on how to respond. Some liberals argue that only peaceful protest is legitimate, while others argue that Antifa's behavior is justified.

Antifa believes that the only means to achieve social equality and to defeat fascists is through violence. However, violent revolution can only be acceptable if the ends justify the means. Antifa groups claim that they act to protect minorities. However, rioting and vandalism only serve to harmfully impact minority communities, as they hurt local businesses, and prevent local employees—who are often members of minorities—from being able to work. While Antifa groups claim the current administration is adopting policies that are harmful to minorities, the government has not yet engaged in violence that justifies the response from Antifa. As long as the political administration remains within the boundaries of the Constitution, any opposition that seeks to go beyond constitutionally allowed measures will be seen as illegitimate. Antifa's violence will only be justifiable to Americans in the face of government-sponsored violence.

Antifa is becoming an important part of a new political resistance, but the organizations will need to decide on long-term political goals that are sustainable within the framework of the US Constitution before they acquire legitimacy. Without long-term political goals, the group will not emerge from its shadow of violence, and will continue to face public opposition from throughout the political spectrum. Antifa must settle on its political motives, or else it risks being overtaken by anarchists and perpetrators of mindless violence. In order for Antifa to achieve real political change, it will need to change its method and goals, or wait for its violent revolution to become truly necessary.

CHAPTER 2

Is the Threat of Fascism Enough to Justify Antifa's Aggressive Tactics?

The Specter of Fascism in American Life

Andrew E. Busch

Andrew E. Busch is a professor of political science at Claremont McKenna College and author of The Constitution on the Campaign Trail: The Surprising Political Career of America's Founding Document.

In the year preceding the August 12 violence in Charlottesville, the term "fascist" was heard more and more frequently in American political discourse. The "Resistance" wasted no time making clear that it saw Donald Trump as fundamentally fascistic. The loose-knit collection of activists known as "Antifa"—short for Anti-fascist—became Trump's most radical and most violent opponents. Others noted fascist tendencies in some of Trump's supporters in the camps of the "alt-right." Others, besieged and harassed by radicals groups including Antifa and Black Lives Matter, have turned the fascist label against their tormenters.

One might have been excused for dismissing such talk as hyperbolic. However, Charlottesville brought into sharp relief the reality that fascism in America in 2017 is not merely a metaphor. If we are to take charges of fascism seriously, we need to think more carefully about what fascism was, in theory and practice. It is not enough to make "fascist" an all-purpose synonym for any outburst of authoritarianism or political violence.

Historical Fascism

Fascism as a movement or a doctrine first emerged in Italy under Benito Mussolini, then spread to many other corners of Europe and Latin America. It took numerous forms, the most virulent of which was German National Socialism, which can be lumped

"Fascism in America?," essay originally appeared in the Claremont Review of Books, by Andrew E. Busch, September 12, 2017. Reprinted by permission.

into the overall fascist phenomenon, but only in certain respects. In others, it must be considered distinctly.

It may be in the realm of conduct that the term "fascist" is most frequently applied today, connoting a thuggish disregard for law and the rights of others and a determination to use force to impose one's will, grounded in hatred and resentment of perceived grievances. The fascists made use of paramilitary squads—such as Italian blackshirts and German brownshirts—who applied intimidation, and who were often armed and eager to engage in violence. The violence both silenced opponents and demonstrated the hollowness of the law, demoralizing the supporters of democracy and leaving a vacuum that the fascists themselves filled. While "brownshirt" tactics are necessary to make a fascist, they are not sufficient. Four aspects of the fascist doctrine also merit attention here.

First, fascism in general and national socialism in particular were collectivist ideologies based on what we might today call racial or ethnic "identity politics." Mussolini left the camp of Marxism-Leninism because he ultimately found communism's collectivist obsession with class less satisfying than a collectivist obsession with nation, defined in group terms as the (Italian) people. National socialism offered an extreme version of this view, focused on an elaborate racial theory in which "Aryans" were good, superior, and entitled to rule, while others were inferior, and at worst either useless or malevolent. As Hitler himself declared in *Mein Kampf,* the folkish state "has to put the race into the center of life in general." As part of its racial doctrine, Nazism was virulently anti-Semitic, more so than most other versions of fascism. Altogether, fascism was a politics based on accident of birth and on group membership. Individual identity, not to mention individual worth or individual rights, had no place.

A second key principle of fascism was the importance of placing unquestioned authority in the hands of a leader. Whether in Germany under Hitler, Italy under Mussolini, or in milder cases such as Argentina under Juan Peron, a cult of personality was created. Again carrying this concept to its furthest extension, the

Nazis lived (and died) by the *fuhrer prinzip*, or "leader principle." The citizen and soldier must, in this view, surrender independent thought to the leader who is the infallible embodiment of the group, as well as to the subordinate leaders who answer to the supreme leader. Hence the first two mandates for party members in the *Nazi Party Organization Book* were "The Fuhrer is always right!" and "Never go against discipline!" German soldiers in 1934 were required to swear an oath not to the German people or to the German constitution, but to Adolf Hitler. To question Hitler, or to challenge the discipline of the hierarchical structure, was tantamount to treason.

Third, both the theory and practice of fascism denigrated rational discourse and celebrated the "will to power." Democracy was condemned largely because it fostered an unending debate in which all ideas were required (and allowed) to compete and to prove themselves with logic and evidence. In order to function, democracy requires freedom of thought and speech. No fascist regime could tolerate that, and every fascist movement did what it could even before taking power to curtail a free exchange of ideas through intimidation. Violence and dogma were elevated to high virtues, replacing empty "parliamentarism." Although opponents called the fascists "reactionary," they saw themselves as progressive, futuristic, and even revolutionary: a new wave of "activism," as Mussolini called it, uninhibited by bourgeois constraints.

Finally but not least, the historic fascist devotion to collectivist identity politics, the leader principle, and the suppression of independent thought all led to a deep hostility to limited government and the free market. Indeed, Mussolini coined the term "totalitarian" to describe his system. "If the XIXth Century was the century of the individual," *Il Duce* wrote, "this is the collective century, and therefore the century of the State…The Fascist State is not a night-watchman." Fascists presented themselves as a third way between Marxist-Leninist state socialism and capitalism. In it, the state might deign to permit continued private ownership of the means of production but only at the price of state control.

Nazi theoretician Ernst Rudolf Huber declared that "The concept of personal liberties of the individual as opposed to the authority of the state had to disappear … All property is common property." Consequently, the Nazis collectivized agriculture, introduced four-year plans, and dictated labor allocations. In both Germany and Italy, fascism was based on state-directed "corporatism," not the free market.

Although each form of fascism manipulated segments of religious opinion to gain support against their avowedly atheistic communist adversaries, fascism was essentially opposed to the Judeo-Christian basis of Western Civilization. Mussolini himself was an atheist, while the attitude of Nazism was summed up in Hitler's personal secretary Martin Bormann's circular to local Nazi Party leaders entitled "National Socialism and Christianity Are Irreconcileable." Fascism's racial/ethnic identity politics was, indeed, fundamentally incompatible with the doctrine of *Imago Dei*, or man created in the image of God. Its virtual deification of the leader and the state, as well as its glorification of violence, were also fundamentally incompatible with basic Judeo-Christian precepts. Recognizing this conflict, varying fascist movements, including the German and Italian, portrayed themselves as alternative "spiritual" phenomena in their own right. "That fascism is vital," Mussolini wrote, "is shown by the fact that it has aroused a faith."

It is not difficult to see a number of similarities between fascism and communism. Both communism and fascism employed violence and intimidation to gain and keep power. Both grounded themselves in a version of collectivist identity politics. Both led in practice to all-powerful dictators supported by cults of personality. Both were enemies of liberty, hostile to the free market, property rights, limited government, and independent civil society. Both saw themselves as "revolutionary" and sought to displace God with a secular religion of totalitarian ideology. Although Mussolini coined the term, totalitarianism—total government control over every aspect of life—was more fully realized in Stalin's Soviet Union or Mao's China than in fascist Italy. Indeed, one might easily conclude that fascism and communism were two versions of the same thing engaged in a bitter family dispute—two overlapping branches of the left wing rather than two opposite things. The similarity between Germany under Hitler and the Soviet Union under Stalin was noted by clear-eyed observers, including such former communists as Arthur Koestler.

Nevertheless, two cardinal theoretical distinctions can be made. Where fascism fixated on race and ethnicity as the basis of collectivism and dehumanization, communism fixated on economic class. Where fascism adopted an explicitly oppositional attitude toward rational discourse, communism purported to be based on scientific principles, even though communists in practice made a mockery of such pretensions.

What Is Antifa Really Anti?

Returning to the present, it goes without saying that the self-professed neo-Nazis in Charlottesville are authentic fascists. One hardly needs to linger over the conclusion that people who give the Nazi salute and chant anti-Semitic slogans are likely to be fascists. Their conduct is undeniably thuggish, and they stand out for the virulence of their white-identity politics, rejection of the norms of reasoned debate, positive embrace of violence, and mindless repetition of 80-year-old German slogans about blood and soil. Their coalition partners in Charlottesville, the neo-Confederates and the alt-right, share in their ignominy.

Once the shock of seeing swastikas in the shadow of Monticello wore off, attention has turned to the neo-Nazis' rivals in combat. Their rhetorical emphasis on equality would seem to place groups such as Antifa and Black Lives Matter outside the philosophical borders of fascism as it is usually understood. And, of course, Antifa stands for "anti-fascist." In their own minds, at least, the idea of their association with fascism must seem ridiculous. Many Antifa activists have openly declared themselves to be communists or anarchists. For that reason, *Washington Post* columnist Marc A. Thiessen has called Antifa "the moral equivalent of neo-Nazis" because he judges them to be communists, and communism to be morally equivalent to Nazism.

In reality, the radical movement, encompassing Antifa, BLM, and others, represents a broad, even amorphous, collection of groups and individuals, and there is not a uniform view among them. It undoubtedly includes many individuals who sincerely believe they are fighting against fascism, racism, or police brutality. However, one can construct a composite of today's radical Left and test it against our checklist of historical fascism. What one finds is that, on balance, today's radicals have much more in common with fascism than most analysts have recognized.

Violence

Radicals have frequently employed violence and force to fight their enemies or to impose their will and silence debate, as noted by political commentators including liberal Peter Beinart and conservative Ben Domenech, who has catalogued over two dozen episodes of violent mob action fomented by the radical left since 2011. Even Nancy Pelosi condemned Antifa by name after its August 27, 2017 rampage in Berkeley. Like fascist violence, Antifa's violence is undergirded both by a calculated goal of undermining order and by raw hate. Bay Area news anchor Frank Somerville reported, after spending time in the midst of the Antifa crowd in Berkeley, "their words were filled with venom, anger, hate, and intolerance ... Hate is hate. And I experienced it first-hand today."

While Antifa openly embraces violence, the Black Lives Matter movement does not. Nevertheless, BLM protests have featured chants calling for violence against police—"pigs in a blanket, fry 'em like bacon"—and several have turned violent in reality, including in Baltimore, St. Paul, Baton Rouge, and Dallas, where a shooter inspired by (though not affiliated with) BLM killed five police officers at the end of a BLM demonstration. Some members of the movement have also been implicated in attempts to silence critical speakers through intimidation and physical force.

Racial Collectivism and Anti-Semitism

The dominant ideological strain among the radicals strives to "put race at the center of life," revolving around collectivist racial identity politics in which individuality is submerged beneath broad racial categories. Accidents of birth are central to this understanding of the human condition, while common humanity or individual worth are denied or downplayed. "White privilege" is the monocausal explanation for everything wrong in the world, and race is often the determinant of how a person is judged. Fascists built racial or ethnic solidarity by promoting resentment and grievance; Black Lives Matter declares that it is "unapologetically black" and "an ideological and political intervention in a world where Black lives are systematically and intentionally targeted for demise."

Antifa apologists like to claim the movement is opposed to anti-Semitism, and note that there are even Jewish Antifa chapters. The website "Fight the New Anti-Semitism" reports, however, that "there is a new trend on American university campuses linking Antifa with BDS," the Boycott, Divestment, Sanctions movement against Israel. Black Lives Matter has also officially endorsed BDS. Of course, it is possible to oppose particular policies of Israel without being anti-Semitic, but the Anti-Defamation League observes that "all too often, BDS advocates employ anti-Semitic rhetoric and narratives to isolate and demonize Israel." Moreover, the objective of BDS—the so-called "right of return" of all Palestinians to Israel—is a transparent attempt to obliterate the State of Israel. In practice, it is almost impossible to separate BDS from anti-Semitism.

Obedience to Leadership

Is individual thought set aside by the radicals in favor of groupthink systematically dispensed and enforced by the movement? There is not yet a single leader figure at the national level (which is true also of the white nationalists), but participants are nevertheless instructed from above on the identities and qualities of a "fascist" or "racist," ever-broadening categories that now include all Trump supporters, capitalists, mainstream but controversial conservatives, police officers, and others. Dissent from the party line is seen as treason and brings swift retribution on social media, a terrifying prospect for the young.

Statism

The radicals are clear opponents of limited government and free markets, preferring instead state control and direction of society, economy, and education (as long as the "right" people are in charge of the state). Antifa has declared capitalists an enemy, and BLM has endorsed an economic program of massive taxation, redistribution, reparations, and government control. The radicals have also focused great attention on education, working to impose an ideological straightjacket on college campuses. It is not yet clear whether this adds up to totalitarianism, but it represents at the least a strong authoritarian streak that accepts no clearly-defined upper limit on state power.

Ideology as Religion

Have the radicals turned their ideology into a secular religion, with its own rituals, dogmatic beliefs, and punishment for heretics? This tendency was noted by numerous analysts after the February 2017 incident at Middlebury College in which social commentator Charles Murray was attacked and a professor injured. At that time, Andrew Sullivan identified the overarching radical ideology of "intersectionality" as a secular religion, and likened the attack on Murray to a scene from *The Crucible* or a "secular exorcism" that reached a "frenzied, disturbing catharsis." Others, such as Peter Beinart, have noted that BLM is harsher and more violent than the civil rights movement of the 1960s partly because, unlike the previous movement, it has largely rejected Christianity in favor of a secular ideology of resentment.

Denigration of Reason

In his article in *New York Magazine*, Sullivan also noted that activists "shut down the [Murray] event because intersectionality rejects the entire idea of free debate, science, or truth independent of white male power." Instead, their ideology explicitly extols emotive themes and *a priori* assumptions. As one Antifa protestor told the newsman Somerville, "We're not interested in talking to you!"

Unlike neo-Nazis, the radicals do not declare in favor of genocide. That feature of national socialism, however, was extreme even among fascists. Moreover, the radicals and their defenders may underestimate the potential long-term danger posed by their toxic cocktail of hatred, racial collectivism, dehumanization and constant broadening of enemies, and self-righteousness. In the end, the radicals share fascistic tendencies on most dimensions. And on the two matters that most distinguish the idea of fascism from the idea of communism—denigration of reason and evidence, and obsession with race—they are nearer to fascism than to communism.

A Campus Demonstration

For evidence, one could consult events in Claremont on April 6, 2017, when journalist Heather Mac Donald was scheduled to speak on the subject of her new book, *The War on Police*. To the radicals, her criticism of BLM was unforgivable. Four days before the talk, a student at Pitzer College created a Facebook event calling for Mac Donald's talk to be shut down. Mac Donald, the student declared, was a racist, fascist, imperialist, and capitalist who must not be allowed to speak. A crowd of around 200 blockaded the event venue, preventing the audience from attending. The talk was live-streamed, though the question and answer period was cut off because police feared the screaming crowd might succeed in breaking into the venue. Mac Donald was then whisked out the back with heavy police escort.

The episode demonstrated the congruence of the radical forces with not just one but nearly every defining feature of fascism. The protestors used physical force, intimidation, and the threat of violence to impose their will and deprive others of their rights to speak, to hear, and to think for themselves. The blockaders embraced race-based identity politics, anti-semitism (made evident by the noticeable selection of anti-Israel signs in the crowd), and statism (one of Mac Donald's crimes, after all, was that she was a "capitalist"). The protest organizers openly dismissed freedom of speech and dialogue among varying viewpoints as meaningless tools of white oppression. Not least, it was doubtful that more than a handful of blockaders had ever read *The War Against Police* or any of Mac Donald's multitudinous other pieces on crime. Indeed, the vast majority had probably never heard of her a week before. They simply accepted the characterization of Mac Donald as a racist and swung into action against her, showcasing the surrender of independent thought and blind obedience to the movement. We have entered the age of the social media gauleiter, commanding the social justice zombie.

Where does this leave us?

At the moment, both white nationalists and radicals are carnival sideshows, aberrations in a country that still, by and large, values peace and freedom. Nevertheless, we are in a place few would have expected a decade ago. One set of newly bold extremists includes self-conscious national socialists as well as other overlapping forces driven by white identity politics. Though covered with a façade of egalitarianism, an alternative extreme has much more in common with the tactics and even philosophical framework of fascism than even it understands. Both groups of extremists seem determined to provoke the other into more and more serious confrontations. A feckless president has contributed to polarization by giving comfort to the alt-right—as his equally feckless predecessor did by endorsing BLM—and seems at a loss when confronted with the consequences. And an increasingly concerned and leaderless center witnesses what looks to some like the unraveling of their country, and are uncertain what to do about it. Weimar America? Not yet. There are even scattered signs that an important corner may have been turned, among them Pelosi's denunciation of Antifa and the suspension of some of the Mac Donald blockaders by Claremont McKenna College. But one fears we are closer to the beginning than to the end of this story.

The Right Is Prepared for Violence and the Left Should Be, Too

Adrian Bonenberger

Adrian Bonenberger graduated from Yale with a BA in English in 2002. He served with the US Army from 2005-2012 as an infantry officer, deploying twice to Afghanistan. He earned a degree in journalism from Columbia and an MFA in creative fiction from SUNY Stony Brook Southampton. He has published numerous articles on the military, national security, and veteran's affairs with a variety of outlets including the New York Times, *the* Washington Post, Foreign Policy, Deadspin, Forbes, *and others.*

Non-violence is morally superior to violence. This is true, and from an ethical standpoint, indisputable. Only an evil person would say otherwise, someone interested in people acting or behaving immorally.

There is, however, a paradox inherent to the pursuit of non-violence. This is evidenced by the pursuit of nuclear weapons by various nations. No country armed with nuclear weapons has ever directly attacked another country armed with nuclear weapons. And the only country to have possessed a nuclear arsenal—Ukraine—was attacked very swiftly after it gave its entire arsenal up (ironically, by the country to which it gave its nuclear arsenal). The greatest act of non-violence almost immediately invited a violent incursion by enemies.

Here is the paradox, then: the only way to ensure non-violence is to be prepared for violence—at least at the level matching one's political (which is to say economic) rivals. It is precisely at the moment that violence becomes a feasible and compelling option when the decision to use non-violence has its greatest moral weight.

In the US, the political left has forgotten this.

[...]

"The Left Must Organize for Violence," by Adrian Bonenberger, The Wrath-Bearing Tree, March 3, 2017. Reprinted by permission.

The Right to Remain Armed

As defined by media and popular imagination, "the right" is a group that encompasses moderate conservatives, libertarians, reactionaries and a hodgepodge of ethnic nationalists and religious extremists.

"The right" believes that national defense comes down to personal responsibility, and that people on the right should personally take responsibility for national defense—actively by being a soldier, or passively by supporting the troops (or at least not passive-aggressively by not supporting the troops or something). A partial consequence of this attitude is that personally taking responsibility for national defense is seen as a positive thing. Another partial consequence of this attitude is that one is encouraged to own weapons—or at least not discouraged from doing so.

Conservatives in US politics and society sees itself as guard against many definitional threats to traditional American values. This often expresses itself as racism, sexism, and homophobia. Because of the intensity of this concern, it also expresses itself in gun ownership. It's worth pointing out here that the executive vice president for the National Rifle Association sees "the left" as a threat on par with radical jihadist terrorism. So much for the NRA's mission to defend the 2nd Amendment and preach the gospel of gun ownership—what they really want is gun ownership *on the right*.

The Right Sees Violence as Valid

Here, we could talk about the structural violence of drug legislation, mass incarceration, police brutality and economic segregation celebrated on the right—of course, centrists (including many Democrats) actively support those phenomena, too. Instead, let's conduct a short thought experiment.

Picture someone on the right expressing their views with a tee-shirt. Chances are, that tee-shirt has an American flag somewhere. It also probably has a gun, or an explicit reference to the necessity of using guns, presumably to protect the flag. It also has some kind of saying like, for example, "don't ever think that the reason I am peaceful is because I forgot how to be violent," (a right wing tee-shirt) or "you may not believe in violence but you are protected by men and women who do" (another right-wing tee-shirt that not subtly encourages its reader to do more to support the troops). It may also say something like "these colors don't run."

Tee-shirts do not an academic or intellectual argument make. But there is a certain truth expressed there, proudly, to be seen by all and sundry in the public square. "The right" understands that violence—verbal, psychological, political, or actual—can be necessary in certain situations. It has prepared itself for this eventuality, ideologically and actually, by encouraging service in the military, by encouraging gun ownership, by encouraging belligerent rhetoric, and by encouraging the wearing of boastful tee-shirts to that effect. It has prepared itself by embracing violence as necessary, valid, essential, and *good*.

"The right" has been wise to do this.

Before the election, I saw evidence of many people on "the right" procuring ammunition and weapons to guard against Hillary Clinton's election. "Cleaning my rifle," one associate from my time in the military posted on his Facebook timeline the day of November 8th (not an uncommon post for a certain demographic). Most people assumed that Clinton would win, and those on "the right" weren't sure what was going to happen next—but they were prepared to use violence if they thought that was necessary.

And not prepared in the sense that they owned guns, and ammunition, and were ready to do something, nebulously connected to violence, maybe, if that was called for. *Cleaning the rifle for use*. Ready and waiting.

What's Left of the US "Left"?

To begin with, the Bill and Hillary Clinton supporters Rush Limbaugh made a career out of attacking, the Obamas and Bloombergs and Rahm Emmanuals that many on the right call "libtards," progressives, liberals, leftists, and commies, are not "the left." They're centrists. Popularly conflated or used synonymously with the Democratic Party, "the left," in US media and popular imagination includes such diverse groups and interests as centrists, moderate liberals, and progressives. They're people with progressive social values, who completely buy into every Ayn Randian notion about how society is and should be structured. They save money and possessions to pass along to their progeny. They exist in the middle and upper middle class, with some exceptions tied to gender and racial identity. They *believe in the American dream.* They think that this dream should be accessible to everyone, regardless of sex, gender, religion, race, or creed.

That's not the left, of course, not even the watered-down US version of "the left" to which Americans became accustomed during the Cold War. The remainder of "the left" that wasn't rooted out by 1950 or so exists now on the fringe—socialists, communists, and the bevy of anarcho-extremist subgroups that one can encounter outside the Democratic Party. There are fewer of them than the Limbaughs and Breitbarters imagine, but more than many Democrats suspected before the 2016 primary.

Differences between subgroups on what most thinkers in the mainstream or salaried media call "the left" and the Democratic Party have been muted by its publicly inclusive nature (at least, up until recently)—moderate conservatives will not dignify neo-Nazi ethno-nationalists with public debate although they share attitudes about trade, for example, but a moderate liberal will debate an anarcho-syndicalist in public or in private, and feel no shame about doing so.

"The left" views physical violence as unacceptable, save occasionally in self-defense. Guns, according to "the left," should not be held or owned by individuals—rather, by groups sanctioned by the government. The state should control the means to violence, and employ it only when faced with some existential threat.

This is almost an exact opposite to how violence operates on "the right," where violence begins as permissible, and the more extreme one becomes, the more enthusiastic the embrace for violence, until one reaches credos like those of the Nazis, which embraced violence and struggle as goods unto themselves.

How Violence on "The Left" Became Taboo

If you repeat the tee-shirt experiment on "the left," it's easy to visualize one of your friends from college or high school wearing a sepia-toned "peace" / "love" / "happiness" style tee-shirt. There are many "Che" tee-shirts, too, but up until Spring 2016, these were less exhortations to violent resistance than knowledge-signaling and fetishistic, exotic aesthetic flourishes among high school and college-age intellectuals dissatisfied with the status quo. According to the norm as it existed before Bernie Sanders' candidacy in the Democratic Primary, wearing a "Che" tee-shirt in college corresponded probably correlated more accurately with a J.D. from Duke, rather than arrest for participation in a radical leftist political group.

The left in America crested with its failed opposition to World War I. When the US became involved, the government passed two acts that permitted crackdowns on anyone preaching disobedience to the war (a group that included the bulk of the left, which saw fighting or dying on behalf of global capitalism as morally wrong). They were called the Sedition Act (1917) and the Espionage Act (1918). While this forced much of the left in the US underground (with increasing aggression and government management after a leftist movement toppled Russia's government in late 1917), their ideas ended up making it into America's economy when the economy collapsed and Franklin Delano Roosevelt became president. McCarthyism, the Cold War, and violent nationalist movements in Russia, and South and Central America that expressed themselves in leftist terms helped drive a nail into its coffin in the 20th century.

The protests against Vietnam were not driven by the anti-war left. The left participated, but for the most part, the movement was co-opted by centrists, and progressives, people from the center-left.

People like John Kerry, and Bill Clinton. Even so, since Vietnam, people who oppose war have been known as hippies, peaceniks, and pinkos.

Use social media instead of the tee-shirt analogy. Taking a position on "the left" means prohibiting violence, giving criminals the benefit of the doubt, and reining in the power of armed individuals. Peaceful protests, peaceful marches, dialogue and empathy versus confrontation.

Violence is wrong, violence is bad, violence is dangerous. People on "the left" understand this. It has been drilled into generations of US citizens—on "the left." What's been forgotten is that the *threat* of violence is a necessary precondition to being taken seriously.

Why Is It Okay for "The Right" to Fetishize Violence, but Not "The Left?"

As with "the left," "the right" is a wide place, and part of it, on the extreme side of the spectrum, is cluttered with gun fetishists, paramilitaries, and people preaching the gospel of violence for violence's sake (often while wearing tee-shirts that attest to this). "The Left"—not so much. Why? Is this a philosophical split, some kind of ideological lens that prohibits violence based on political attitudes?

I believe it goes back to the USSR's founding—the Russian revolution, and the seizure of massive amounts of private property by "the left" in various countries, part of a doomed attempt to usher in Karl Marx's utopian visions through force. This coincided with "the left" in America gathering a great deal of actual political and economic power, in the form of unions, anti-capital populist politicians, and isolationists who wanted to keep the US out of World War I entirely. So much so that the center and right formed an alliance to destroy the left—permanently.

That catastrophic neutering was so deep, so profound, and lasted with no break for so long, that it takes historical research to dredge up simple facts like, for example, a major presidential candidate (Eugene Debs) was imprisoned under the aforementioned

Sedition Act from 1917-1921… *by a Democrat.* Or that between 1880 and 1930, thousands of workers were killed while striking by police, National Guardsmen, and hired guns in the employ of businessmen. Murdered, not beaten (though beaten, too). That, in fact, innocent people were executed for having appeared to conform to the national narrative of the dangerous and destabilizing, revolutionary left.

At least they got a trial.

Newspapers eagerly reprinted stories of leftist violence and agitation in the US, eager to forestall what they saw as a likely revolution on the part of workers, along the lines of what had happened in Russia. Many former Russian nobles were here to offer testimony about the horrors of the Russian Revolution (one assumes they left out the details of how their treatment of serfs could possibly have led to this eventuality), and business owners in the US were already outraged about the having lost political or social leverage. A scapegoat was found for all: American socialists. The American left.

Even the moderate socialism of Franklin Delano Roosevelt was deemed heretical by later generations of centrists eager to accommodate "the right." Instances of socialism among Republicans, carefully censured and controlled (though brought up when expedient), like Eisenhower's interstate-building project, or Nixon's development of the Department of Housing and Urban Development. Socialism, the redistribution of wealth, was an absolute bad—was un-American. One didn't get political concessions from *violence*, on the left—one got it through making deals, in a free market of political ideas.

For a time at the end of WWI, nothing in the US was more dangerous than an armed worker taking part in any kind of collective bargain. Not even an armed black man offered a greater threat, and everyone knows that an angry, politically motivated armed black man is the most terrifying image to large swaths of the US public (and especially the voting public). No, it was the specter of workers seizing power that led Hoover to order MacArthur and Patton to charge and break up the "Bonus Army" of WWI vets clamoring for assistance in Washington, DC.

A Way Forward

But this does not mean that "the left" cannot turn things around. On the contrary, "the left" can and should begin militarizing, immediately. By taking back the means of violence that is every American's Constitutional right, "the left" will be able to bargain again on its own terms—or, failing that, expose centrists as the collaborationist stooges they are, and "the right" as fascists, elitists, despots and authoritarians.

Arming for violence requires the following actions, which conscientious and politically committed leftist must carry out at the earliest opportunity. 1) leftists must join the military, with special attention to the combat branches. Joining the Army Infantry and the Marine Corps, becoming Navy SEALs, and Army Rangers, and Green Berets, and Explosives Ordnance Disposal Technicians in any branch must be priorities for leftists. Pilots of helicopters and fighter jets, too, are critically important. 2) leftists must buy, train on, and maintain rifles, carbines, and handguns. 3) leftists should organize into groups of 10-15, and do activities like (2) together.

Organizing for violence does not mean that "the left" should or will initiate violence, anywhere. Non-violence is and must remain a solid, core tenet of what it means to reside on the intellectual or political left, along with humanism and a belief that in spite of our fundamentally flawed nature, generosity is necessary, even with enemies. I was witness to the efficacy of this behavior during both deployments to Afghanistan—as well as the necessity of having force behind the non-violence.

Non-violence is the means by which the left can carry out political opposition—this is where moral superiority exists. But it cannot happen without arms—assault rifles, sniper rifles, pistols, and the means to fabricate more and greater means for destruction.

IEDs, pipe-bombs, and all manner of devices should be within the left's means—if not its possession (those things that are not legal to possess should not be possessed).

If "the left" is unarmed, if it does not know the ways of war and warfare, it will gain and retain nothing. Its political opposition figured this out a long time ago.

Repeated by people on the right and at the center, even by progressives, the assessment that the left is incapable of backing its rhetoric up with anything save non-compliance (which is easily corralled through arrest, imprisonment, and economic sanction) is correct. There is no coercive means the left could use beyond mean words—not even hypothetically—and for those who adore and respect violence as an effective means of dispute resolution, this means there is no reason to grant them any special consideration.

Without weapons, training, and resolve, the left will be given exactly and precisely nothing. Which means, on a certain level, that the left *deserves* nothing.

Rather than discussing the various ways in which people on the left can protest, or organize, or collaborate, it is more useful today to discuss how to prepare a substantial portion of patriotic, loyal US citizens using just and strong leftist political ideology for military service.

The Psychology of Right Wing Authoritarianism

Magnus Lindén

Magnus Lindén is an associate professor at Lund University. His research interest lies in the psychological aspects of aggression, abuse, and human rights violations, especially in connection to armed conflicts and terrorism. Dr. Lindén has, among other things, investigated risk factors of pro-torture attitudes in the war on terrorism, and he is currently working with the Swedish military investigating "dark" personality traits and battlefield ethics in the Swedish peacekeeping force deployed to Mali.

Since the horror of Hitler's Holocaust, psychologists have investigated why certain individuals appear more prone to follow orders from authority figures, even if it means that they have to sacrifice humanitarian values while doing so.

Apart from the Nazi regime, this issue is central to military atrocities such as the massacre in My Lai during the Vietnam war, and the systematic abuse of detainees in Abu-Ghraib prison in post-invasion Iraq.

But it also applies to civilian situations such as the recent unethical behaviour of some members of the US border control in the aftermath of Donald Trump's executive order to ban Muslims entry to the country. Handcuffing a five-year-old child is not what you would necessarily consider "normal" human behaviour. Yet it happened.

While this issue has been debated on and off for decades, scientific research suggests that some people's personality make-up gives them strong authoritarian and anti-democratic tendencies. That is, they either support or follow orders from authorities even when these orders could harm—or increase the risk of harming—other human beings.

After World War II, leading researchers, including Theodor Adorno and Else Frenkel-Brunswik at the University of California in Berkeley, were interested in understanding how ordinary German people could turn into obedient mass murderers during the Nazi genocide of the Jewish population in Europe.

Using research on ethnocentrism as a starting point and basing their work on clinical studies, they built a questionnaire with the overall aim of mapping the antidemocratic personality. The scale, called the F-scale (F stood for fascism), focused on aspects such as anti-intellectualism, traditional values, superstition, a willingness to submit to authorities and authoritarian aggression. An individual scoring highly on the scale was labelled an "authoritarian personality."

Unfortunately, the F-scale turned out to be methodologically flawed which limited its use for understanding authoritarianism.

Racist, Sexist, Aggressive, Gullible

In the early 1980s, Bob Altemeyer, a professor at the University of Manitoba, refined the work with the F-scale and came up with a new definition of the authoritarian personality. Altemeyer renamed the authoritarian personality "right-wing authoritarianism" (RWA) and defined it as having three related dimensions. These were: a submission towards authorities, endorsement of aggressive behaviour if sanctioned by authorities, and a high level of conventionalism—that is conforming to old traditions and values.

Among antisocial traits and attitudes investigated in psychology, RWA definitely ranks high up the naughty list. Right-wing authoritarians are, for example, more racist, more discriminatory, more aggressive, more dehumanising, more prejudiced and more sexist than individuals with low RWA. They are also less empathic or altruistic. Another downside is that they tend to think less critically, instead basing their thoughts on what authority figures say and do.

Research findings also suggest that those with high RWA are more likely to follow unethical orders. For example, in a replication of the famous Milgram obedience experiment in a video environment, high RWAs were found to be willing to use more powerful electric shocks to punish their subjects.

Scoring high on RWA is theoretically in line with the anti-democratic personality suggested by Adorno and his colleagues. A plethora of studies shows that people with these traits are more anti-democratic—for example, they tend to support restriction of civil liberties and surveillance, capital punishment, the mandatory detention of asylum seekers and the use of torture in time of war.

Threat to Democracy

So can RWA pose a threat for a democratic society? The answer is generally speculative, but at least hypothetically the answer could be yes. Some indications of its potential danger can be found in the following fields of research.

A study on university students has shown that the level of authoritarian attitudes is significantly higher immediately after a terrorist attack than during a non-threatening condition. This supports findings from longitudinal research showing that RWA increase when the world is perceived to be becoming more dangerous.

How such reactions relate to people's political choices has suddenly become very relevant. Researchers interested in understanding destructive political leadership suggest that one must look at how environmental conditions, the followers and the leader interact with each other. This is what is referred to as the toxic triangle—a society with a high degree of experienced threat, a narcissistic or hate-spreading political leader and followers with unmet needs or antisocial values is at risk of adopting a destructive political course.

So it's unsurprising to hear that authoritarianism was found to be one of the factors statistically predicting support for Donald Trump before the recent US election.

Not only this but experimental data suggest that those displaying high RWA are more prone to be supportive of unethical decisions when they are promoted by a socially dominant leader—that is, a leader viewing society as a hierarchy in which domination of inferior groups by superior groups is legitimised.

Researchers in this area have suggested that individuals scoring high on RWA, and other antisocial traits and attitudes, are more likely to choose occupations in which the opportunity to be abusive to others might arise. Based on this reasoning, one could expect that soldiers and police officers should have a higher level of RWA than comparison groups. And this appears to be borne out by research that suggests that both soldiers and border guards have higher levels of RWA in comparison to the rest of the population.

How these findings relate to actual abusive behaviour remains to be investigated in future research. But the idea of having people with these traits guarding a democracy seems to me to be something of a contradiction in terms.

When Political Institutions Fail to Contain Fascist and Far Right Movements, Aggressive Opposition Becomes a Moral Necessity

Natasha Lennard

Natasha Lennard is a contributing writer at the Intercept. *Her work covers politics and power and has appeared in* Esquire, *the* Nation, *and the* New York Times *opinion section. Her book* Violence, *co-authored by Brad Evans, will be published in 2018.*

To call Trumpism fascist is to suggest that it demands from us a unique response. We *can* deploy the "fascism" moniker to Trump's ascendance by recognizing features like selective populism, nationalism, racism, traditionalism, the deployment of Newspeak and disregard for reasoned debate. The reason we *should* use the term is because, taken together, these aspects of Trumpism are not well combated or contained by standard liberal appeals to reason. It is constitutive of its fascism that it demands a different sort of opposition.

Liberals cling to institutions: They begged to no avail for faithless electors, they see "evisceration" in a friendly late-night talk-show debate, they put faith in investigations and justice with regards to Russian interference and business conflicts of interest. They grasp at hypotheticals about who could have won, were things not as they in fact are. For political subjects so tied to the mythos of Reason, it is liberals who now seem deranged. Meanwhile, it is the radical left—so often tarred as irrational—who are calling upon both US and European histories of anti-fascist action to offer practical and serious responses in this political moment. For all the ink spilled about rising fascism, too little has been said about anti-fascism.

Anti-fascist, or antifa, doesn't only delineate that which opposes fascism. It is a set of tactics and practices that have developed since the early 20th century (and the rise of fascism in Italy) as a confrontational response to fascist groups, rooted in militant left-wing and anarchist politics. As organizers from anti-fascist research and news site Antifa NYC told *The Nation*: "Antifa combines radical left-wing and anarchist politics, revulsion at racists, sexists, homophobes, anti-Semites, and Islamophobes, with the international anti-fascist culture of taking the streets and physically confronting the brownshirts of white supremacy, whoever they may be." As with fascisms, not all anti-fascisms are the same, but the essential feature is that anti-fascism does not *tolerate* fascism; it would give it no platform for debate.

The history of anti-fascism in 20th-century Europe is largely one of fighting squads, like the international militant brigades fighting Franco in Spain, the Red Front Fighters' League in Germany who were fighting Nazis since the party's formation in the 1920s, the print workers who fought ultra-nationalists in Austria, and the 43 Group in England fighting Oswald Mosley's British Union of Fascists. In every iteration these mobilizations entailed physical combat. The failure of early-20th-century fighters to keep fascist regimes at bay speaks more to the paucity of numbers than the problem of their direct confrontational tactics.

A more recent history of antifa in both Europe and the United States illustrates the success these tactics can have, particularly when it comes to expunging violent racist forces from our neighborhoods and defending vulnerable communities, while also creating networks of support that do not rely on structurally racist law enforcement for protection against racists. Anti-fascist tactics focused primarily around physical force proved effective in forcing neo-Nazi groups out of entire neighborhoods in Europe and the United States in the 1980s. Back then, as longtime organizer and member of the Industrial Workers' World General Defense Committee (GDC) Kieran Knutson told *The Nation*, fascist and anti-fascist formations grew out of youth subculture scenes. Taking on and largely defeating neo-Nazi gangs, multi-racial crews of anti-racist skinheads and punks coalesced and grew into semiformal Anti-Racist Action (ARA) chapters nationwide. "At its peak, in an era without cell phones or internet, ARA had over 100 chapters across the US and Canada," explained Knutson, adding that students, older leftists, feminists and more joined efforts to counter a broader group of racist organizations, from the white power music scene to KKK rallies. The network faded in the 2000s, drifting in part to the anti-globalization movement, but as Knutson "the several thousand veterans of this movement are still out there—many still involved politically in anti-racist, feminist, queer, labor, education and artistic projects."

The need for this sort of community and street resistance will not be contingent on Trump carrying out repressive policies—the emboldening of far right racists is a *fait accompli*. At the end of November, the Southern Poverty Law Center released a report documenting nearly 900 separate incidents of bias and violence against immigrants, Latinos, African Americans, women, LGBT people, Muslims and Jews in the ten days that followed Trump's win.

Physical confrontation is just a small aspect of antifa direct action, but the history of anti-fascist, anti-racist action is not one of so-called allies standing in polite disapproval or donning safety pins. "Fascism is imbued with violence and secures itself politically through the use or threat of it, so it is inevitable that anti-fascists have to countenance some involvement in violence themselves," wrote M. Testa, author of *Militant Anti-Fascism: A Hundred Years of Resistance*.

The ability to "countenance" some involvement with violence is itself a privilege that so many people of color and LBGTQ individuals in this country cannot enjoy—violence is not countenanced but systematically thrust upon them. The question of whether the counter-violence should be a tool of resistance in the Trump era will no doubt cleave some anti-Trump unities currently breaching the liberal center, the left, and far left. Those of us who long before Trump have defended counter-violence against oppression—as in Ferguson, as in Baltimore, as in Watts, as in counter-riots against the Klu Klux Klan, as in slave revolts—

know where we stand. The number of people willing to engage with explicitly anti-fascist organizing and rhetoric has certainly increased with Trump's rise, "As an empirical measure, our Twitter followers have almost quadrupled from the beginning of this year," organizers for NYC Antifa told me via e-mail, "new groups are popping up everywhere, and we are fielding requests from all over the country about how to get involved." Whether this means a significant number of people are willing to engage in anti-fascist physical confrontation in Trump's America remains to be seen.

"We don't think it's useful to rehash the same old [violence versus non-violence] arguments," NYC Antifa noted. "If Trump tries to register Muslims and engage in mass deportations, a Change.org petition is not going to stop it." (Indeed, mass deportations and the mass surveillance of Muslims under the Obama administration would not have ended with a petition either.)

But the old canard of violent versus non-violent protest is already finding a new locus in debates around whether or not to give the racist far right a platform. When neo-Nazi Richard Spencer at his National Policy Institute held their annual conference in DC last November, anti-fascist activists exposed the event, its attendees, and where its members were dining, and attempted to not only protest but disrupt and shut down the conference, as well as Spencer's dinner plans (succeeding, at least, in dousing the white nationalist in "a foul smelling liquid). News and monitoring sites like NYC Antifa, Anti-fascist News and It's Going Down have been reporting on the NPI, exposing their members and their conferences since before Trump's candidacy. "Now that Steve Bannon, who has positioned himself as a champion of the alt-right, is heading to the White House, the NPI's seig-heiling and fashion sense is a trending topic covered by most major media outlets," NYC Antifa noted, "Yet, for the most part, all these journalists do is reproduce Spencer's sentiments, which he frames in liberal rhetoric to gain appeal, and feign outrage. Our approach is to expose and confront them."

The forms of physical force that served against neo-Nazis in the street in the 1980s are harder to deploy against the contemporary suit clad neo-Nazi holding a conference with professional security details, or a position in the White House. It will be an uphill battle to beat the alt-right in the dromological battlefield of social media resonance. For one, fascism lends itself to meme form, as fascist form itself purports to give a simple solution to a complex problem; memes aren't inherently fascist, of course, but their reductive format is well-suited to fascist content. Leftists have reductive phrases and catchphrases, too, and no one would diminish the popularity of Birdie Sanders. But weaponizing meme form is, I believe, easier for a political project that itself takes the form of reduction and over-simplification.

The antifa task, I believe, is not to make better memes, but to expose the fascists behind the Pepe avatars, reveal their connections, and chase them away. Committed neo-Nazis deserve no more privacy than they deserve public platforms, or safety, even though antifa groups have been known to grant second chances. "We've had success with this tactic, and have gotten people to leave groups who did not want to be publicly shamed," the NYC Antifa organizers told *The Nation*. "One guy's boss was Jewish and he didn't want it known he was working with Holocaust deniers. We took him off our website after he promised to leave the group he was in. We believe second chances are important—our goal is to get people to leave racist and fascist movements."

The alt-right might not seek us in the streets, and might trounce us in trolling, but disruption, confrontation, doxxing and altercation remain tactics anyone taking seriously a refusal to normalize Trump-era fascism should consider. Liberals who reject such a strategy in defense of the right to free of speech and assembly engage in an historical NIMBYism, in which only in the past, or in other countries, has militancy against white supremacy been a legitimate resistance. They forget, too, that while the First Amendment ensures that the government will not interfere with free speech, this has no bearing on neo-fascists having the right to be heard or countenanced by the rest of us. For the radical left, no such bad thought takes hold, because militant tactics against white supremacy never stopped being necessary—in the fight against slavery, Jim Crow, red-lining, and mass incarceration—with or without explicit white nationalists in center political stage.

As a recent statement from Antifa NYC noted, "Before the election, collectives in different cities were organizing in support of people dealing with exploitative bosses and slumlords, With larger participation, these networks could become increasingly viable in a post-Trump world." Founded by a cadre of activists in New York who grew close during Occupy in 2011, anarchist community space, The Base, opened three years ago as a hub for autonomous organizing around prisoner solidarity, offering support for local residents facing abuse and coercion from landlords, reading groups, self-defense trainings, and more. Following Trump's victory, the number of people joining their projects has skyrocketed.

Eight months ago, a number of organizers from The Base launched the Rapid Response Network, which aims to establish neighborhood groups, connected via a hotline, that can provide safety, first aid, and assistance in the event of Immigration and Customs Enforcement raids on undocumented individuals, as well as a physical presence and defense from in the event of racist street attacks. Such networks have been a staple of anti-fascist, militant anti-racist organizing—deployed by anti-state groups from the Black Panthers to the Anti-Racist Action skinheads battling an upsurge in neo-Nazi gang violence in the 1980s. "When we held our first training meeting, 15 people turned up. Since the election that number has quadrupled. Two hundred people have expressed interest on Facebook for the next session. We've had to find a bigger venue and add sessions" a Rapid Response Network organizer and founder who goes by Layla told *The Nation*. (It is common for anarchist and antifa groups, eschewing individualism and facing harassment from active neo-Nazi groups to refuse to give full names to the press; I'm respecting that here).

Alongside efforts like the Rapid Response Network, which focuses on neighborhood defense, activist collectives are working with interfaith groups and churches in cities around the country to create a New Sanctuary Movement, continuing and expanding a 40-year-old practice of providing spaces for refugees and immigrants, which entails outright refusal to cooperate with ICE. Anti-fascist mobilizations are forming voluntary networks like Community Action Team NYC (CATNYC) which are willing to travel to different neighborhoods and physically confront the rising tide of racist violence and harassment.

Since networks like RRN and CAT are still in their developmental stages, Trump's inauguration is an opportunity—with regards to spectacle—to set the tone of resistance to come. On January 21, the day *after* the inauguration, an expected 200,000 people are expected to march in DC in the "Women's March," which, according to original organizers is "not a protest" but an effort to "send a bold message to our new administration on their first day in office, and to the world that women's rights are human rights," which they (wrongly) suggest "transcend politics." It will be a show of solidarity and togetherness, a presence far better than an absence. A policy platform released by march organizers last week offers a progressive and strong message of intersectional feminism. However, a procession of hundreds of thousands of people moving through barricaded streets carrying props and banners can be easily forgotten and ignored—the most historically large marches in recent history have failed to pass muster in history making beyond their size alone. When the status quo is not threatened, its upholders tend not to listen. We rallied in our peaceful millions against the Iraq War, too. The Women's March nevertheless promises to bring thousands of people together—at worst a liberal parade, at best a jumping of point for the necessary work of local organizing to begin. If it is not a site of protest, I hope it will still be a place of politicization.

Meanwhile on January 20, the call for the actual inauguration day is unequivocal protest. More than 50 anarchist, anti-fascist, anti-racist groups from across the country have called for a #J20 Disruption. "We call on all people of good conscience to join in disrupting the ceremonies. If Trump is to be inaugurated at all, let it happen behind closed doors, showing the true face of the security state Trump will preside over," the announcement reads, "We must take to the streets and protest, blockade, disrupt, intervene, sit in, walk out, rise up, and make more noise and good trouble than the establishment can bear. The parade must be stopped. We must delegitimize Trump and all he represents." One member of the "DC counter-inaugural welcoming committee" commented anonymously that housing space for 1,000 visiting radicals, in both church halls and houses, had been organized by their group alone. New York anarchists are raising funds to rent whole buses to attend. And, as historic anti-fascist mass protest dictates, there are plans for a large black bloc—a spectacle both intentionally threatening and anonymizing. The expectation of altercation with Trump supporters who will also descend on DC is high.

The different approaches to the Inauguration suggest a cleaving in responses to Trump along well worn liberal, liberal-left and radical-left fault lines when the need to build political alliances is urgent. The decision to join the Women's March or Disrupt #J20 should not be a benchmark for division. This line instead should only be drawn when someone, in professed name of democracy, would sooner condemn or even imprison anti-fascist, anti-racist actors before they would see a ceremony affirming and buoying fascism meet with interference.

Authoritarianism Is a Threat to America and Decentralized Movements Are Necessary to Defeat It

Maria J. Stephan and Timothy Snyder

Maria J. Stephan is the co-author of Why Civil Resistance Works: The Strategic Logic of Nonviolent Conflict *and the co-editor of* Is Authoritarianism Staging a Comeback? *Timothy Snyder is the Housum Professor of history at Yale University. An expert on Eastern Europe and the Second World War, he has written several books, including* Black Earth: The Holocaust as History and Warning *and will soon publish* One Tyranny: Twenty Lessons from the Twentieth Century.

After the spread of democracy at the end of the 20th century, authoritarianism is now rolling back democracy around the globe. In the US, supporters of democracy disarmed themselves by imagining an "end of history" in which nothing but their own ideas were possible. Authoritarians, meanwhile, keep practicing their old tactics and devising new ones.

It is time for those who support democracy to remember what activists from around the world have paid a price to learn: how to win.

Modern authoritarians rely on repression, intimidation, corruption and co-optation to consolidate their power. The dictator's handbook mastered by Orban in Hungary, Erdogan in Turkey, Maduro in Venezuela, Zuma in South Africa, Duterte in the Philippines and Trump here provides the traditional tactics: attack journalists, blame dissent on foreigners and "paid protestors," scapegoat minorities and vulnerable groups, weaken checks on power, reward loyalists, use paramilitaries, and generally try to reduce politics to a question of friends and enemies, us and them.

"Authoritarianism Is Making a Comeback. Here's the Time-tested Way to Defeat It," by Maria J Stephan and Timothy Snyder, Guardian News and Media Limited, June 20, 2017. Reprinted by permission.

Yet tyrants' tactics require the consent of large numbers of people. The first lesson, then, is not to obey in advance. If individuals make the basic effort to consider their own sense of values and patriotism rather than subconsciously adjusting to the new reality, aspiring authoritarians have a major problem. Good citizens will then ask: but what should we do? History provides an answer: civil resistance.

Unarmed civilians using petitions, boycotts, strikes, and other nonviolent methods have been able to slow, disrupt and even halt authoritarianism. Civil resistance has been twice as effective as armed struggle. Americans will remember the historical examples of Gandhi and Martin Luther King, and perhaps the peaceful east European revolutionaries of Solidarity in Poland and Otpor in Serbia. Many of us have overlooked the more recent examples of successful civil resistance in Guatemala, South Korea and Romania.

Civil resistance works by separating the authoritarian ruler from pillars of support, including economic elites, security forces, and government workers. It attracts diverse groups in society, whose collective defiance and stubbornness eventually elicits power shifts.

Mass, diverse participation empowers reformers and whistle-blowers and weakens the support base of hardliners. The best gauge of the health of a resistance movement, then, is whether the size and representativeness of active participation are growing.

Civil resistance is strategic. Movements articulate clear, achievable goals (achieving independent trade unions in the case of Solidarity; de-segregating public places during US civil rights movement) and knowint when and how to declare small victories. They must endure inevitable set-backs—like arrests, large counter-mobilizations by regime supporters, and legislative defeats—while maintaining momentum.

Movement organization can take different forms, but decentralized leadership rooted in local communities is more important than charismatic leaders. The Serbian Otpor movement combined centralized planning with de-centralized tactical adaptation and recruitment.

The organizing approach of Harvard lecturer Marshall Ganz, which emphasizes building cross-sector relationships and turning resources into the power needed to achieve clear goals, highlights how to build resilient movement infrastructure over the long haul.

Movements that devise and sequence a broad repertoire of tactics, including those that bring people together for concentrated actions (rallies, sit-ins, blockades) and those that involve dispersed acts of resistance (consumer boycotts, stay-aways, go slow tactics), are more likely to endure and grow.

Repeating the same tactics is boring, predictable, and unlikely to move the needle. Gene Sharp has identified 198 methods of nonviolent action grouped according to the level of risk, preparation, and forcefulness associated with them.

Authoritarian regimes often seek to provoke violence by opposition elements in order to justify repressive counter-measures. Nonviolent movements have invested in training, they have devised codes of conduct and designated marshals to enforce nonviolent discipline at protests. Scholars have found that the stronger the organization of a movement, the more likely it is to avoid responding to violence with violence, which weakens the resistance by decreasing the level of citizen participation.

Successful movements need to be able to inspire hope and optimism in order to sustain popular participation in the resistance and focus people on building alternative systems. Authoritarians thrive on popular fear, apathy, resignation, and a feeling of disorientation. Movement leaders need to assure people that their engagement and sacrifices will pay off, something Solidarity leader Adam Michnik understood well: "Above all, we must create a strategy of hope for the people, and show them that their efforts and risks have a future."

Supporters of democracy have access to immense resources, in dozens of languages, on strategic applications of civil resistance and movement building. These include films, manuals, books, articles, databases of global nonviolent campaigns, and organizations that specialize in online and offline training and mentoring.

In the United States, the resistance is strong. Older civil rights organizations like the ACLU have stepped up their legal game and are starting to invest in grassroots people power training and activities. New structures, like the over 6,000 local Indivisible groups across the country, are channeling citizen outrage and depression into constructive forms of putting pressure on members of Congress at town halls and in their offices. The Women's March mobilized the single-largest demonstration in American history.

Social trust is strengthening between movement leaders and organizations. Over 50 major organizations and movements representing a variety of issues, including environmental rights, economic justice, immigrant rights and anti-racism, formed a United Resistance campaign and vowed to treat an attack on one as an attack on all.

Another social change collective, The Majority, brings together activists, organizers, and groups with different missions. Meanwhile, sanctuary cities are popping up across the US to protect undocumented immigrants from forceful arrest and deportation. Federal workers are enrolling in trainings to learn their legal rights and discuss ways to serve ethically.

The question of "what can I do" has answers, supported by scholarship and experience. Authoritarianism always begins with the advance obedience of the thoughtless and the disorientation of the thoughtful. But we know that we should act, and we know how.

The American Left Is Degrading Itself by Engaging in Violent Tactics

Albert Eisenberg

Albert Eisenberg is a Philadelphia-based digital marketer and communications specialist. He previously served as Communication Director for the Philadelphia GOP.

H amburg, Germany, July 2017. As world leaders gather for the G20 summit, far-left "anti-fascist" (Antifa) rioters set fire to cars and property, terrorize residents, and injure more than 200 police officers attempting to keep the peace. Did you miss it? CNN's initial reports referred to the "protesters" as "eclectic" and "peaceful."

But you need not cross the shining seas to experience violence, destruction of property and a general dismantling of liberal values from the political left. You could simply visit America's elite college campuses like Yale or Middlebury or Berkeley, where tomorrow's leaders attempt to shut down conservative voices with protest or riots. At Middlebury, rioting students landed liberal professor Allison Stranger in a neck brace for the crime of defending a conservative academic's right to speak. At Berkeley, mobs of students created a "war zone" ahead of a planned visit from conservative provocateur Milo Yiannopoulos, injuring Trump supporters and causing $100,000 in damages.

Or head to Portland, Oregon, one of the most liberal cities in the nation in the heart of the progressive Pacific Northwest, which last week Politico labeled "America's Most Politically Violent City." The progressive paradise—where Republicans are virtually an extinct species—has witnessed millions in damages attributed to the same types of anti-fascists-in-name-only that kept Hamburg residents paralyzed in fear this month. A "counter-protest" to a

"Commentary: Liberal America Has a Political Violence Problem," by Albert Eisenberg, Philadelphia Media Network (Digital), LLC, July 18, 2017. Reprinted by permission.

planned pro-Trump rally landed 14 Antifa in jail for attacking the police with explosives and bricks.

Witness the blood-soaked Congressional baseball field in Alexandria, Virginia, site of the June attack on Congressman Steve Scalise (R-LA) and other Republicans batting up for their annual bipartisan game. James Hodgkinson, a "fervent supporter of progressive politics," showed up to the field with a rifle, and handgun, and a hit list of Republicans. As Scalise fought for his life, MSNBC host Joy Reid felt conflicted: the attempted assassination was a "delicate thing" because of Scalise's conservative viewpoints like opposition to gay marriage. "Are we required in a moral sense to put that aside in the moment?" she wondered. (My response? Yes, Joy, you are. The shooting of a mainstream, leadership Republican Congressman is completely reprehensible, and it's not justifiable.)

Now cross the Potomac and visit the halls of Congress, where Democratic lawmakers have accused Republicans of murder for supporting an overhaul to the spiraling, ruined ObamaCare program, which by next year will leave dozens of counties without a single option for insurance. Reasonable people can disagree about how much our Medicaid program should grow without comparing the Republican bill to 9/11, as Bernie Sanders did last week. Or saying the healthcare bill is paid for with "blood money" of dead Americans, as Elizabeth Warren tweeted shortly after the Scalise attack. If our sitting Senators don't act more responsibly, who will?

Instead of retweeting, liberals who care about preserving our political system should be outraged that these are the standard-bearers of their party.

Nobody is directly responsible for a shooting except the shooter, and nobody throws a brick except the person who picks it up. No side has a monopoly on political violence. There are loonies at the fringes of every political movement—mentally ill, perturbed and paranoid—who can be stirred towards violence or dissuaded from it. But when we have Democratic Senators accusing political opponents of murder, when our college campuses descend into assault zones for conservative speakers (or those that defend them), when our major cities become playgrounds for far-left rioters and the media glosses over it, we move towards a more violent and fractured society, not a safer one.

If gay people were pouring into bars and punching straight people, I as a gay man would speak out. If Jews were propagating terror in the name of our religion, I would condemn it vociferously. And when violence has come from the conservative side, I don't hesitate to stand against it. But it's not. There have been no right-wing groups storming campuses and flinging feces at speakers we don't like; no tea party mobs destroying property, assaulting police officers and paralyzing residents of our major cities; and no Republican Senators calling their colleagues murderers just weeks after a political assassination. From Portland to New Haven to Washington, DC, the violence we're witnessing is largely a product of the hard left, and the reaction from mainstream liberals—mostly silence, dismissiveness, equivocation—means it will continue to flourish.

To move toward a less violent and hyper-charged society, we must be clear-headed about violence where we see it, and not avoid the subject. We must condemn it without conditions.

If you think Republicans are murderers, you're an extremist. If you're trading in that kind of rhetoric just to shut the other side up or raise a buck, you're giving cover to extremists. And if you object to political violence but fail to speak out, your weakness is causing our society to fracture. It's time for liberal America to speak out against violence and the rhetoric that incites it.

Left Wing Violence Is Out of Control in the United States

Jacob Grandstaff

Jacob Grandstaff is a PhD candidate at the University of North Alabama and a freelance journalist whose work focuses on institutional and governmental policies that affect millennials.

Left-wing domestic terrorism has increased at alarming rates since the 2016 election under the auspices of an underground radical movement that calls itself "Antifa," or "anti-fascist action." Much of this violence has been centered around Portland, Oregon, where Antifa guerrillas have assaulted peaceful demonstrators and conservative groups in the name of combating an ever-expanding definition of fascism.

In April 2017, the 82nd Avenue of Roses Business Association in Portland cancelled its annual Rose Festival and parade because it received an anonymous email allegedly from Antifa groups threatening violence if the Multnomah County Republican Party was allowed to participate in the parade. The email noted ominously: "You have seen how much power we have downtown and that the police cannot stop us from shutting down roads so please consider your decision wisely ... This is nonnegotiable."

This isn't the first instance of fascistic action by so-called anti-fascist groups.

In Sacramento, California in June 2016, hundreds of Antifa rioters attacked 30-odd members of the white nationalist Traditional Worker's Party (TWP). Although CRC does not support the goals of the TWP, the group had obtained a lawful permit to demonstrate when Antifa protesters violently refused to allow the group to express its First Amendment rights. In the ensuing melee, fourteen

From "Antifa: The Resurgence of Left-Wing Street Warfare," by Jacob Grandstaff, Capital Research Center, August 8, 2017. Reprinted by permission from Capital Research Center.

people received stab wounds, and two were sent to the hospital in critical condition (they both survived).

After the incident, the Sacramento County District Attorney's office filed a 2,000-page report listing 514 misdemeanors and 68 felonies involving 101 people—relating to everything from unlawful assembly to assault with a deadly weapon. Nevertheless, only three of the Antifa counter-demonstrators have been arrested. Police cite the fact that many of the counter-demonstrators wore masks as the reason for not being able to apprehend more of the assailants.

Yvette Felarca, a former middle school teacher, was one of those arrested. Felarca is a member of the radical pro-illegal immigration outfit "By Any Means Necessary," an Antifa splinter group that participated in the February 2017 shutdown of a speech by conservative activist Milo Yiannopoulos at the University of California, Berkeley. In quintessential Stalinist fashion, Felarca argued that local business owners whose stores were vandalized by the Antifa guerrillas should direct their ire at Berkeley's Chancellor, Nicholas Dirks, for allowing Yiannopoulos to speak in the first place—rather than the terrorists who destroyed their businesses. She further defended the blatant attack on free speech in a subsequent interview: "I was there… it was a militant protest and everyone was there to shut him down." The Left, she argued, has been "far too timid for far too long"—which led to "someone like Donald Trump leading a fascist movement."

Felarca's comments are revealing.

The ethos unifying factor these disparate and violent Antifa groups is the belief that the Republican Party and President Donald Trump are fascist. As Peter Beinart notes in *the Atlantic*, an overwhelming percentage on the American Left believe Trump is a racist. Trump's presidency, they hold, promotes "fascist undertones" and "hateful rhetoric;" thus convinced that Trump and his supporters were raging fascists bent on the Nazification of the US, these largely unknown, mostly internet-based Antifa activists took to the streets to terrorize legitimate conservative opposition and shut down free speech.

The establishment Left has offered limited criticism of Antifa's anarchist tactics, so long as the group aims its attacks at perceived white supremacists. When a masked Antifa activist punched the white supremacist Richard Spencer in the face on Inauguration Day, *Slate* praised the assault and *the Nation* called it an act of "kinetic beauty." But Antifa has gone far beyond confining its attacks to white supremacists and fringe conservative groups. Its activists genuinely believe President Trump is a fascist and as such, vilify anyone who supports him or the Republican Party.

If Donald Trump and his supporters truly are fascists, then it only makes sense for his opponents to use "any means necessary" to stop his administration. In reality, however, the Trump's election represents a disastrous spoke in the wheels of the radical Left's agenda—and convinced many Left-wing anarchists that they can't rely on the ballot box to "fundamentally transform the United States of America" as former President Barack Obama put it.

"America Under Siege: Civil War," the first part in a series produced by Dangerous Documentaries, the film-wing of Capital Research Center, exposes the goals of organized Leftist groups to disrupt President Trump's inauguration and presidency, and the terrorist tactics their violent foot soldiers employ to that end.

The United States Is Experiencing a Major Political Crisis and Antifa Is Making Things Worse

Diana Johnstone

Diana Johnstone is an American writer based in Paris. Her work focuses on European and American politics. Previously, she was European editor of the US weekly magazine In These Times *from 1979 to 1990.*

A historic opportunity is being missed. The disastrous 2016 presidential election could and should have been a wakeup call. A corrupt political system that gave voters a choice between two terrible candidates is not democracy.

This should have been the signal to face reality. The US political system is totally rotten, contemptuous of the people, serving the corporations and lobbies that pay to keep them in office. The time had come to organize a genuine alternative, an independent movement to liberate the electoral system from the grip of billionaires, to demand a transition from a war economy to an economy dedicated to improving the lives of the people who live here. What is needed is a movement for the pacification of America, at home and abroad.

That is a big order. Yet this approach could meet with wide support, especially if vigorous young people organized to stimulate popular debate, between real live people, from door to door if necessary, creating a mass movement for genuine democracy, equality and peace. This is as revolutionary a program as possible in the present circumstances. A moribund left should be coming back to life to take the lead in building such a movement.

Quite the opposite is happening.

"The Harmful Effects of Antifa. Crisis of America's Left," by Diana Johnstone, GlobalResearch.ca, October 24, 2017. Reprinted by permission.

Provoking a New Civil War?

The first step toward preventing such a constructive movement was a false interpretation of the meaning of the Trump victory, massively promoted by mainstream media. This was essentially the Clintonite excuse for Hillary's loss. Trump's victory, according to this line, was the product of a convergence between Russian interference and the votes of "misogynists, racists, homophobes, xenophobes, and white supremacists." The influence of all those bad people indicated the rise of "fascism" in America, with Trump in the role of "fascist" leader.

In this way, criticism of the system that produced Trump vanished in favor of demonization of Trump the individual, making it that much easier for the Clintonites to solidify their control of the Democratic Party, by manipulating their own leftist opposition.

The events of Charlottesville resembled a multiple provocation, with pro- and anti-statue sides provoking each other, providing a stage for Antifa to gain national prominence as saviors. Significantly, Charlottesville riots provoked Trump into making comments which were seized upon by all his enemies to brand him definitively as "racist" and "fascist." This gave the disoriented "left" a clear cause: fight "fascist Trump" and domestic "fascists." This is more immediate than organizing to demand that the United States end its threats against Iran and North Korea, its open and covert project to reshape the Middle East to ensure Israel's regional dominance, or its nuclear buildup targeting Russia. Not to mention its support for genuine Nazis in Ukraine. Yet that trillion dollar policy of global militarization contributes more to violence and injustice even in the United States than the remnants of thoroughly discredited lost causes.

The Left and Antifa

All those who are sincerely on the left, who are in favor of greater social and economic equality for all, who oppose the endless aggressive foreign wars and the resulting militarization of the American police and the American mentality, must realize that, since the Clintonian takeover of the Democratic Party, the ruling oligarchic establishment disguises itself as "the left," uses "left" arguments to justify itself, and largely succeeds in manipulating genuine leftists for its own purposes. This has caused such confusion that it is quite unclear what "left" means any more.

The Clintonian left substituted Identity Politics for the progressive goal of economic and social equality, by ostentatiously coopting women, blacks and Latinos into the visible elite, the better to ignore the needs of the majority. The Clintonian left introduced the concept of "humanitarian war" to describe its relentless destruction of recalcitrant nations, seducing much of the left into supporting US imperialism as a fight for democracy against "dictators."

Antifa contributes to this confusion by giving precedence to the suppression of "bad" ideas rather than to the development of good ones through uninhibited debate. Antifa attacks on dissidents tend to enforce the dominant neoliberal doctrine that also raises the specter of fascism as pretext for aggression against countries targeted for regime change.

Antifa's Excuses

Antifa has several favorite arguments to justify itself those who criticize its use of force and intimidation to silence its adversaries.

1. Its violence is justified by the implicit violence of its enemies who if left alone plan to exterminate whole groups of people.

2. This is demonstrably untrue, as Antifa is notoriously generous in distributing the fascist label. Most of the people Antifa targets are not fascists and there is no evidence that even "racists" are planning to carry out genocide.

3. Antifa is engaged in other political activity.

4. That is completely beside the point. Nobody is criticizing that "other political activity." It is the violence and the

censorship which are the hallmarks of the Antifa brand, and the target of criticism. Let them drop the violence and the censorship and get on with their other activities. Then nobody will object.

5. Antifa defends threatened communities.

6. But that is certainly not all they are doing. Nor is that what its critics are objecting to. Actual defense of a truly threatened community is best done openly by respected members of the community itself, rather than by self-styled Zorros who arrive in disguise. The problem is the definition of the terms. For Antifa, the victim community can be a whole category of people, such as LGBTQI, and the threat may be a controversial speaker at a university who could say something to hurt their feelings. And what community was being defended by Linwood Kaine, younger son of the Democratic Party Vice Presidential candidate, Senator Tim Kaine, when he was arrested in St Paul, Minnesota, last March 4 on suspicion of felony second-degree riot for attempting to break up a pro-Trump rally at the State Capitol? Although Kaine, dressed in black from head to toe, resisted arrest, the matter ended there. What downtrodden community was the young Kaine defending other than the Clintonite Democrats? His own privilege as a family member of the Washington political elite?

7. Antifa claims that it is in favor of free speech in general, but racists and fascists are an exception, because you can't reason with them, and hate speech is not speech but action.

8. This amounts to an astounding intellectual surrender to the enemy. It is an admission of being unable to win a free argument. The fact is that speech is indeed speech, and should be countered by speech. You should welcome the chance to debate in public in order to expose the weaknesses of their position. If indeed "you can't reason

with them," then they will shut down the discussion and you don't have to. If they resort to physical attack against you, then you have the moral victory. Otherwise, you're giving it to them.

9. Antifa insists that the Constitutional right to free speech applies only to the State. That is, only the government is banned from depriving citizens of the right to free speech and assembly. Among citizens, anything goes.

10. This is a remarkable bit of sophistry. Bullying and intimidation are okay if done by an unofficial group. In keeping with neoliberalism, Antifa is out to privatize censorship, by taking over the job itself.

Verbal Violence

The verbal violence of Antifa is worse than their physical violence insofar as it is more effective. The physical violence is usually of minor consequence, at most temporarily preventing something that will happen later. It is the verbal violence that succeeds most in preventing free discussion of controversial issues.

Alarmed by the proliferation of pro-Antifa articles on CounterPunch, I ventured to write a critique, *Antifa in Theory and Practice*. My criticism was not personal; I did not mention the authors of those pro-Antifa CounterPunch articles and my mention of author Mark Bray was respectful. The result was a torrent of vituperation on CounterPunch's FaceBook page, as well as in a hostile email exchange with star Antifa champion Yoav Litvin. This culminated with a hit piece by Amitai Ben-Abba published on CounterPunch itself. Note that both Litvin and Ben-Abba are Israelis, but pro-Palestinian, which provides the two with impeccable left credentials.

These reactions provided a perfect illustration of Antifa discussion techniques. It is a sort of food fight, where you just throw everything you can pick up at the adversary, regardless of logic or relevance. On the FaceBook page, Litvin, on the basis of my past carefully objective articles on French politics, accused me of "shilling for Marine Le Pen." Irrelevant and inaccurate.

In his hit piece Ben-Abba dragged in this totally off-topic assertion:

> "Much in the same way that her early '00s pseudo-historical denial of the massacre in Srebrenica worked to embolden Serbian nationalists, her present analysis can embolden white supremacists."

Need I point out that I never denied the "massacre" but refuse to label it "genocide," nor did Serbian nationalists ever need my humble opinion in order to be "emboldened"—especially since the war was over by then.

I happily grant that there are issues raised in my initial article that deserve debate, such as immigration or whether or not the "fascism" of the early twentieth century still exists today. Indeed my whole point was that such issues deserve debate. That's not what I got. Ben-Abba came up with this imaginary allusion to the immigration issue:

> "Antifa" is a broader umbrella term that allows formerly unaffiliated folks (like the sans-papiers migrant baker who makes Johnstone's croissants) to participate in defense of their communities against neo-fascist intimidation."

Very funny: I am exploiting some poor undocumented baker and preventing him from being defended. Aside from the fact that I very rarely eat a croissant, the bakers in my neighborhood are all fully documented, and moreover this largely immigrant neighborhood is the scene of frequent peaceful street demonstrations by African *sans-papiers* clearly not intimidated by neo-fascists. They obviously do not need Antifa to protect them. This fantasy of omnipresent neo-fascism is as necessary to Antifa as the fantasy of omnipresent anti-Semitism is to Israel.

Antifa rhetoric specializes in non sequitur. If you agree with some conservative or libertarian that it was wrong to destroy Libya, then you are not only guilty of association with a pre-fascist, you are a supporter of dictators and thus probably a fascist yourself. This has been happening in France for years and it's just getting started in the United States.

The Antifa specialty is labeling anti-war activists and writers as "red-brown," red for left and brown for fascist. You may pretend to be on the left, but if we can find the slightest association between you and someone on the right, then you are a "red-brown" and deserve to be quarantined.

By claiming to defend helpless minorities from a rising fascist peril, Antifa arrogates to itself the right to decide who is, or might be, "fascist."

Whatever they think they are doing, whatever they claim to be doing, the one thing they really are doing is to tie the left into such sectarian intolerance that any broad inclusive single-issue anti-war movement becomes impossible. Indeed, it is precisely the imminent danger of nuclear World War III that leads some of us to call for a non-exclusive single issue anti-war movement—thus setting ourselves up as "red-brown."

That is why Antifa—unwittingly let us say—is running interference for the war party.

It is most unfortunate to see CounterPunch become a platform for Antifa. It didn't have to. The site is quite able to reject articles, as it has systematically rejected contentions about 9/11 or as it rejected David Cobb's and Caitlin Johnstone's (no relative) right to respond. It could have taken a principled stand against calls for violence and censorship. It did not do so. It is one thing to encourage debate and quite another to sponsor mud wrestling.

Antifa Is Undermining the Efforts of Peaceful Activists on the Left

Mitchell Zimmerman

Mitchell Zimmerman is an intellectual property attorney in San Francisco. He was a civil rights worker with the Student Nonviolent Coordinating Committee in the South in the 1960s.

Y ou can't trust anyone over 30," some of us used to say in the 1960s. Now that I'm over 70—and still struggling for social justice—I see there are people under 30 you cannot trust: the supposed "Antifa" (anti-fascist) groups that have, in effect if not in intent, become the secret little friends of Fox News and, ironically, American fascism.

I don't speak lightly. We've seen it before: young people whose infatuation with violence undermines the progressive cause.

In the 1960s, we fought effectively and nonviolently against American apartheid and against America's mass killing in Vietnam. I was an organizer in eastern Arkansas for the front-line civil rights group Student Nonviolent Coordinating Committee (SNCC) and an anti-Vietnam War organizer, speaker and author, arrested a number of times in both pursuits.

Enormous numbers of people came to support those nonviolent movements. But we had our Antifas, too. They called themselves "Weathermen," and they claimed we needed to "bring the war home."

They brought street fighting with the police and further violence to our otherwise peaceful anti-war actions. They undermined broader participation and gave political ammunition to pro-war forces. They helped elect Richard Nixon, prolonging the war for years.

"Progressives Cannot Prevail by Tolerating Antifa's Violence," by Mitchell Zimmerman. This op-ed was originally published by Mitchell Zimmerman on Sept. 1, 2017 in the *Daily Californian*. Reprinted by permission..

Sadly, the same violent, self-obsessed mentality is at work today.

In response to the widespread condemnation of Trump after Charlottesville, white supremacists sprang to his defense, proposing pro-Trump demonstrations in Berkeley, among other cities.

On Sunday, I joined 4,000 others at a Berkeley counterprotest. A myriad of signs proclaimed Berkeley's rejection of hate and white supremacy and expressed support for immigrants, people of color and other targets of Trumpian rage. But among the peaceful demonstrators were dozens of black-clad, masked Antifa, a frightening sight as they marched in a menacing phalanx.

They claim they were there to defend themselves and others. But, commonly, there is no violence at protests when they don't appear, and when they do, their macho warrior posturing provokes violence even when they don't actually initiate it.

At Berkeley, a hundred members of Antifa crossed police barriers to assault the Trump supporters. Not surprisingly, the violence of this handful won more media attention than the message of the peaceful thousands.

Their assault was profoundly misguided. Violent efforts to suppress or expel white supremacists can only weaken and harm the movement to defend democracy.

The rightists need to be tolerated—and, indeed, should have been protected—not because their speech is innocuous, but because suppression is worse.

First, attacking them changes the subject of contention from their racism to our tactics. Do we want people discussing the right's pathetic defense of Confederate heroes—or our violence against them?

Second, violence feeds the Fox News and Breitbart storyline that progressives are enemies of freedom. Just as Weathermen helped the GOP convince middle America that opposition to the Vietnam War was an unpatriotic fringe activity, the Antifa antics promote the falsehood that leftist violence is the main problem, not resurgent white supremacy.

Third, Antifa confrontations—even their combative appearance—discourage participation by masses of people who don't want to be caught in a riot. The Women's Marches following Trump's inauguration had a giant impact because millions took peacefully to the streets. That impact would have been completely undercut had a handful of militants wreaked acts of violence in the name of "anti-fascism."

Fourth, if it is deemed acceptable in Berkeley that local police need not protect those whose views are deemed hateful and repugnant, that same principle will cut against us elsewhere in America and will be said to justify ignoring violence against progressive speakers, particularly in places where, for example, local politicians claim Black Lives Matter is a "hate" group with a violent anti-police ideology.

Finally, if political violence becomes the norm, the fighting won't be limited to fists, sticks and Mace. After all, which side has the guns?

Antifa thinks only of its immediate satisfaction in expressing anger. But politics is not just about self-expression. It is about effecting change, and this requires influencing millions of people who don't presently agree with us. The political theater of Berkeley is playing on the larger stage of America, where Antifa's militant posturing and self-indulgent violence does grave damage.

However they may think of themselves, Antifa is actually just what the right-wing ordered. Its tactics have no place in the struggle to defend American democracy.

Does the Antifa Model Provide a Constructive Blueprint for the Future of the Left?

Antifa's Impact on Contemporary American Politics

J.P. Green

J.P. Green is a writer for the Democratic Strategist. *His work focuses on electoral and campaign politics in the United States.*

The resistance to the Trump Administration's assault on civil and human rights includes the emergence of a controversial group known as "Antifa," whose participants have made it clear that they have no objection to using physical violence to challenge hate groups. Most recently, Antifa was highly-visible at the Charlottesville protests, in which a young woman was killed by an auto driven by a right-wing terrorist.

"Antifa is short for anti-fascists," writes Jessica Suerth at cnn. com. "The term is used to define a broad group of people whose political beliefs lean toward the left—often the far left—but do not conform with the Democratic Party platform. The group doesn't have an official leader or headquarters, although groups in certain states hold regular meetings." There is a longer tradition of anti-fascist resistance groups in Europe and elsewhere.

As Peter Beinart notes at *The Atlantic,*

> The movement traces its roots to the militant leftists who in the 1920s and 1930s brawled with fascists on the streets of Germany, Italy, and Spain. It revived in the 1970s, 1980s, and 1990s, when anti-racist punks in Britain and Germany mobilized to defeat Neo-Nazi skinheads who were infiltrating the music scene. Via punk, groups calling themselves anti-racist action—and later, anti-fascist action or antifa—sprung up in the United States. They have seen explosive growth in the Trump era for an obvious reason: There's more open white supremacism to mobilize against.

"Does the 'Antifa' Movement Help or Hurt the Democratic Cause?" by J. P. Green, The Democratic Strategist, August 16, 2017. Reprinted by permission.

As members of a largely anarchist movement, antifa activists generally combat white supremacism not by trying to change government policy but through direct action. They try to publicly identify white supremacists and get them fired from their jobs and evicted from their apartments. And they disrupt white-supremacist rallies, including by force.

Antifa in the US is really more of a loose aggregation of resistance groups, most of whom share a general belief that progressives should not shrink from returning the violence committed by Klan, neo-nazis or other Alt-right groups. Judging by news videos, the Antifa does appear to be growing in size, which is understandable, given the uptick in hate group activity. Brenna Cammeron reports at bbc.com that the closest thing Antifa has to a web page, the "It's Going Down" website received around 300 hits daily in 2015, now garners between 10-20,000 hits a day."

Brian Levin, director of the Center for the Study of Hate and Extremism at California State University, San Bernardino, said of the Antifa in Suerth's article, "What they're trying to do now is not only become prominent through violence at these high-profile rallies, but also to reach out through small meetings and through social networking to cultivate disenfranchised progressives who heretofore were peaceful."

Beinart argues that "some of their tactics are genuinely troubling." Specifically,

They're troubling tactically because conservatives use antifa's violence to justify—or at least distract from—the violence of white supremacists, as Trump did in his press conference. They're troubling strategically because they allow white supremacists to depict themselves as victims being denied the right to freely assemble. And they're troubling morally because antifa activists really do infringe upon that right. By using violence, they reject the moral legacy of the civil-rights movement's fight against white supremacy.

However, adds Beinart, "saying it's a problem is vastly different than implying, as Trump did, that it's a problem equal to white supremacism. Using the phrase "alt-left" suggests a moral equivalence that simply doesn't exist … Antifa's vision is not as noxious. Antifa activists do not celebrate regimes that committed genocide and enforced slavery."

According to the Anti-Defamation League, Beinart writes, "right-wing extremists committed 74 percent of the 372 politically motivated murders recorded in the United States between 2007 and 2016. Left-wing extremists committed less than 2 percent." Few rational swing voters are likely to be convinced that violence from the political left is as pervasive as that from the right.

Suerth reports that "White nationalists and other members of the so-called alt-right have denounced members of Antifa, sometimes calling them the "alt-left," which Trump repeatedly referred to in his widely-criticized remarks yesterday at Trump Tower.

Antifa supporters might argue that a little physical confrontation of the Brooks Brothers Rioters back in 2000 might have prevented a lot of human misery. They also believe that, when a neo-fascist knows that they can easily be on the receiving end of violence, they will temper their behavior.

But opening the door to violent resistence is a more dangerous strategy in that there are millions more guns circulating today than back in the mid-late 1960s, when progressives debated the choice between violent and nonviolent methods for social change. Despite the mass shooting in Alexandria, what is remarkable is how few incidents have occurred in which the perpetrator of violence can be accurately identified as a left-progressive of any sort. How long can this last in a society increasingly poisoned by social anger and the unrestricted proliferation of assault weapons?

Going forward, it seems a sure bet that Trump and the Republicans, particularly their alt-right flank, will make broad-brush characterizations of the American left as violent. Trump's Tuesday rant is a signal that this strategy, which appears to have Bannon's fingerprints, is already being implemented. They will hold up the example of the mass shooting in Alexandria, VA that wounded US Rep. Steve Scalise as corroborating evidence that the left is as violent as the right, and they will have the bully pulpit and GOP echo chamber to parrot this false equivalence meme. Many will believe them and many others will take the bait just because it fits their comfort zone with their families and friends.

I imagine that many of the Antifa protesters are admirers of Martin Luther King, Jr. But those who would follow Dr. King should remember his insistence that "means and ends must cohere." Had Dr. King at any juncture legitimated violent resistance to injustice, his credibility would have been squandered, and we would be living in a very different nation. It's an impressive tribute to his leadership and the dedication of his S.C.L.C. staff and coworkers in the Civil Rights Movement that this principle was never compromised, even when they were being brutalized and murdered by racists.

Adhering to an exclusively nonviolent strategy is not about basking in the glories of ideological purity. It is every bit a strategic consideration. As King often pointed out, nonviolence confers a unique credibility and dignity on its practitioners. When an individual is assaulted and refuses to return the violence as a matter of principled self-discipline, witnesses of the incident, which today could be many millions of television and internet viewers, will be moved toward a profound emotional sympathy with the victim and antipathy towards the perpetrator.

Thus far Antifa has not been very violent, at least in comparison to the alt-right. But they should take care not to project an overly violent spirit, which is easily captured on video and in photos and can be amplified and exaggerated in different media formats. It wouldn't hurt to give more thought to the optics of yelling threats and brandishing sticks. They can be made to look more violent than they are in reality.

Regardless of the direction the Antifa chooses, now would be a good time for progressive groups who espouse exclusively nonviolent means to proclaim and amplify their uncompromising commitment to their principles. Enduring credibility is more likely to come from consistent nonviolence than physical retaliation.

Antifa's Small-Scale Violence Pales Next to the Large-Scale Threat of Fascist and Far Right Movements

Paul D'Amato

Paul D'Amato is managing editor of the International Socialist Review *and author of* The Meaning of Marxism *(Haymarket Books, 2006).*

After big mobilizations against Nazi hate in Boston and the Bay Area last month, there has been a flurry of denunciations of violence.

Not far-right violence, though. Instead, the attacks are against those committed to stopping the Nazis.

As hard as it is to believe after the string of assaults committed by members of white supremacist organizations, culminating in the murder of Heather Heyer in Charlottesville, Virginia, Democratic Party politicians like Nancy Pelosi are echoing Donald Trump in denouncing the "violent actions of people calling themselves Antifa."

This is not only an exaggeration of the violence of anti-fascists and an underestimation of the qualitatively more aggressive violence of the far right. It is also a false equation, because it fails to distinguish between the actions of those seeking to commit atrocities against millions of people, and those committed to stopping such atrocities from taking place.

Among anti-fascists, there are debates about how to build a movement to stop the rise of a menacing and dangerous far right—and those debates are extremely important.

But we cannot confuse this debate with the attacks on the left by political figures—themselves complicit in creating the social conditions that have given rise to right-wing extremism—who place protective police cordons around fascists and restrict the rights of those resisting them.

"In Defense of Anti-fascism," by Paul D'Amato, SocialistWorker.org, September 15, 2017. Reprinted by permission.

Before the violent "unite the right" rally in Charlottesville, politicians and the media routinely equated the "alt-right" and the "alt-left." The press acted almost as an echo chamber for the far right when it claimed that its rallies were for "free speech" and that it only showed up at protests with weapons to "defend" itself against the left.

This narrative helped the far right build wider legitimacy. Indeed, some Democrats denounced the "alt-left" long before Trump and the right used it as a smear. As Sam Kriss writes in *Politico*:

> The invention of the alt-left allowed centrist liberals to pretend that ... [t]hey were sandwiched between two sets of frothing fanatics who secretly had a lot in common with each other. It established their particular brand of liberalism, possibly encompassing a few "moderate Republicans," as the only reasonable ground, besieged by alts.

Charlottesville—and Trump's response—put a temporary stop to this enabling chatter. Millions across the country were stunned when hundreds of alt-right, pro-Confederate, Klan and neo-fascist thugs wielded torches, clubs, pistols and assault rifles, along with flags and shields emblazoned with Klan and Nazi symbols, and chanted openly anti-Semitic, Nazi slogans like "Jews will not replace us" and "Blood and soil."

A Klan leader fired his pistol into a crowd of anti-fascists, groups of white supremacists attacked and beat several counterprotesters, and another fascist used his car as a weapon to murder Heather Heyer and injure many more.

According to David Z. Morris writing in *Fortune*, well before the rally, "attendees were planning for violence," sharing "advice on weaponry and tactics, including repeatedly broaching the idea of driving vehicles through opposition crowds."

Trump's response was to complain that his far-right supporters in Charlottesville were being "treated unfairly," and to condemn "both sides"—as if "to somehow pretend," writes Kriss, "that the murderousness of the Nazis and the Klan is no worse than the people forced to defend themselves against it."

The national revulsion against Trump's outbursts put pressure on the president to denounce the far right—but he reverted to form the next day and complained about the behavior of the "alt-left."

For the first time since the far right got wind in its sails from Trump's election, the national discussion was overwhelmingly around how the fascists must be categorically denounced. Even archconservatives felt compelled to denounce the far right. "We should call evil by its name," said Republican Sen. Orrin Hatch. "My brother didn't give his life fighting Hitler for Nazi ideas to go unchallenged here at home."

The outrage against the attack in Charlottesville also produced an outpouring of protest, as thousands turned out to counter planned far-right rallies in Boston, Knoxville, Tennessee, the Bay Area and elsewhere, outnumbering the white supremacists by as many as 100 to one, as well as producing momentum in cities across the South to take down Confederate statues. In the Bay Area and elsewhere, many of the scheduled racist rallies were canceled.

These protests showed that the *starting point* for building momentum and defeating the far right is drawing out large numbers of people to oppose them.

It was inevitable, though, that mainstream politicians—liberal and conservative—would soon revert back to a narrative condemning the fascists and anti-fascists equally.

After thousands came out to protest the far right in Berkeley, routing a handful of white supremacists who turned up despite their rallies being canceled, a whole host of officials, from House Minority Leader Nancy Pelosi to the Mayor Jesse Arreguin of Berkeley, took the opportunity to condemn the anti-fascists. Arreguin said that the "uniformed" Antifa should be treated as a "gang," and that all protesters, violent or not, should be held "accountable."

Even some associated with the left, like Chris Hedges, took the opportunity to denounce Antifa.

Hedges wrote that these anti-fascists and the far right "mirror each other" and recommended that, rather than confronting the fascists, their opponents should take the advice of the Southern Poverty Law Center and "[h]old a unity rally or parade to draw media attention away from hate." He did, however, agree that there is "no moral equivalency between Antifa and the alt-right" and that the state is merely using the "false argument of moral equivalency to criminalize the work of all anti-capitalists."

The argument that fascists and anti-fascists are the same because both use violence is a false equivalency that willfully fails to understand the nature of the far right. The terror in Charlottesville is part of a pattern of activity designed to legitimize white supremacy and to "normalize" violence, terror and intimidation.

There is a thread that connects the nooses found hanging in front of the Smithsonian in Washington, DC, and on the Oakland waterfront; the nine murders committed by Dylann Roof in a Black church in Charleston, South Carolina; the stabbing death of Richard Collins III in College Park, Maryland, at the hands of a member of "Alt Reich: Nation"; the killing of two men who intervened to stop racist harassment on a Portland train by Jeremy Joseph Christian; and James Field ramming his car into the crowd of anti-fascist demonstrators that included Heather Heyer—whose death is the first instance in recent history of a white supremacist committing murder during a political demonstration.

These incidents are part of a pattern that reveals the true nature and intent of the extreme right in the US. All of the killers were either members or supporters of racist, white supremacist organizations that target Blacks, non-European immigrants, women, Muslims, Jews and LGBTQ people. The aim of these organizations is the creation of an all-white United States—in the words of Richard Spencer, an "ethno-state for all Europeans."

The history of lynching and Klan terror in the South, and of Hitler's "final solution" in Germany, should remind us that these forces aim to organize a mass movement with racist, genocidal aims.

The more they are able to spread and normalize their ideas, the more they create conditions in which they are emboldened to gather in ever-larger numbers and commit ever more violent outrages.

Condemnations of violence by US officials are hollow hypocrisy. The nonprofit group Airwars calculated that at least 3,100 civilians were killed in Iraq and Syria by US-led air strikes from August 2014 to March 2017. In one week in August, 26 Afghan civilians were killed in US and NATO air strikes.

It is the purest hypocrisy for someone like Nancy Pelosi, a staunch defender of the deployment of American military might overseas, to say that "we must never fight hate with hate," and that "peace" represents "the best of America."

Whenever any politician says that "violence is not the answer," we have to ask why the United States has the most militarized police forces in the world, known throughout the world for their brutality against Black, Brown and poor people.

In an act of coordinated national violence, Barack Obama directed city police forces across the nation to forcefully shut down the Occupy movement. Every president has engaged in overseas military action that has led to the deaths of hundreds, sometimes thousands, sometimes hundreds of thousands—and, in the case of the Korean and Vietnam wars, millions of people.

The ruling class has no problem with violence—so long as it's deployed in its own interests. What it doesn't like is when ordinary people take a stand against oppression and violence.

A distinction should therefore be made between the violence of the oppressor and the oppressed. As the Russian revolutionary Leon Trotsky once wrote, "A slave owner who through cunning and violence shackles a slave in chains, and a slave who through cunning or violence breaks the chains— let not the contemptible eunuchs tell us that they are equals before a court of morality!"

Among those who genuinely hate fascism, some have made the case against the use of *any* force, even in self-defense, against fascists. For example, Julian Brave NoiseCat writes in an August

31 *Guardian* op-ed article, "Violent tactics, even if they are only deployed sparingly and defensively, undermine the resistance."

It isn't clear how defending ourselves against the violence of the far right would undermine us. Quite the contrary, what undermines us is what fascists thrive on: the ability to intimidate and instill terror as a means of controlling public spaces.

Heather Heyer took a stand against violent racism and xenophobia, and she paid the ultimate price. If it had been possible for someone, through the use of physical force, to stop the car that killed her, would that have been justified? Absolutely.

Those who say that, in principle, all violence is equal are saying something absurd: that the Jew who resists the concentration camp is the moral equivalent of the fascist who tries to put her there.

Violence does not necessarily degrade those who use it. The abolitionist Frederick Douglass believed that when escaped slaves used force to prevent a slave-catcher from forcibly returning them to bondage, they were helping to lift slaves up from both physical and mental bondage. On the contrary, for Douglass, it was the persistent lack of resistance in the face of unremitting oppression that had the most morally degrading effect on the oppressed.

Logan Rimel, a parish administrator at University Lutheran Chapel of Berkeley, who traveled to Charlottesville to bear witness to the far-right rally, wrote that the Antifa "protected a lot of people that day":

> I've seen a lot of condemnation of "violent response," lots of selective quoting Dr. King, lots of disparagement of Antifa and the so-called "alt-left," a moral equivalency from the depths of Hell if I ever saw one. You want to be nonviolent? That is good and noble. I think...I do, too. But I want you to understand what you're asking of the people who take this necessary stance against white supremacy, the people who go to look evil in the face. You're asking them to be beaten with brass knuckles, with bats, with fists. To be pounded into the ground, stomped on, and smashed. You're asking them to bleed on the pavement and the grass. Some of them are going to die. And you're asking them to do that without defending themselves.

Clearly the police won't defend us against the violence of the far right. In all the recent confrontations, they have protected and defended fascists and "alt-right" forces, creating a protective cordon around them wherever they gather under the guise of defending their "free speech" rights. Meanwhile, various restrictions on free speech and assembly are imposed on progressives and leftists who oppose them.

In Charlottesville, the police and National Guard stood by and watched as heavily armed neo-Nazis harassed, attacked and, in at least one instance, shot at anti-fascist protesters. ProPublica's A.C. Thompson, who was in Charlottesville, reported about how, in a "scene that played out over and over," police "watched silently from behind an array of metal barricades" as:

> an angry mob of white supremacists formed a battle line across from a group of counter-protesters, many of them older and gray-haired, who had gathered near a church parking lot. On command from their leader, the young men charged and pummeled their ideological foes with abandon. One woman was hurled to the pavement, and the blood from her bruised head was instantly visible.

According to Alan Zimmerman, president of the Congregation Beth Israel in Charlottesville, police failed to provide guards when the synagogue requested it. Meanwhile, writes Zimmerman, "For half an hour, three men dressed in fatigues and armed with semi-automatic rifles stood across the street from the temple."

Zimmerman reported that, "Several times, parades of Nazis passed our building, shouting, 'There's the synagogue!' followed by chants of 'Sieg Heil' and other anti-Semitic language. Some carried flags with swastikas and other Nazi symbols."

At the anti-fascist protest of 4,000 in Berkeley last month—the one that prompted Nancy Pelosi's outburst against "Antifa"—the university, city and state police arrived in full force, clad in riot gear, erected concrete barricades around the planned protest site, deployed rooftop snipers, and banned everything from backpacks to fruit.

Police recklessly drove motorcycles through the rally space and attempted to block protesters from reaching Martin Luther King Jr. Civic Center Park, the site where the far right had intended to rally. The cops did nothing, moreover, to prevent a handful of far-right provocateurs from harassing the rally from beginning to end.

In Boston, police set up two sets of barricades and a cordon of officers to protect the far right protesters and safely escorted them away from their rally site in police prisoner transports, striking anti-fascist protesters with clubs to clear a path. According to the *Intercept*, the organizer of the right-wing rally, John Medlar, posted on his Facebook page that the Boston Police "literally saved our lives" and that he couldn't thank them enough.

You couldn't imagine a statement like that coming from Black Lives Matter protesters, May Day marchers or workers on a picket line. The lesson here is clear: We can't rely on the state to stop the far right. They are enablers of the rightists, and any tool we hand over willingly to them, ostensibly to stop the fascists, will be used against our side.

That doesn't mean that there are not important question regarding how best to organize against the rise of the far right. The disagreement with Black Bloc tactics articulated in previous *SW* articles is a disagreement over the best means of fighting the fascists, not a preference for pacifism versus violence.

The key to a successful fightback, as the counterdemonstrations in the Bay Area and Boston show, begins with the largest and broadest mobilization of all the forces repulsed by fascism—which represents the vast majority of the population. These mobilizations show tangibly that we will not be intimidated and create the political climate that makes the far right think twice about bringing out their forces.

Anti-fascism is reduced to a spectator sport if left to groups of masked, armed activists who do battle with groups of (usually better-) armed fascists.

What we do not need is the method that sees larger protests, in the words of one defender of Black Bloc tactics, Arlo Stone, as "incubation opportunities for [the] Black Bloc to form and destroy property." Mass protests should be seen as part of a broader assembly of forces to confront the fascists, not as a medium allowing Black Bloc the cover and anonymity to engage in a cat-and-mouse confrontation with police.

In the context of mass mobilization, we must be prepared to confront and defeat the fascists. But the defense of our organizations, our movements and our demonstrations should be a coordinated effort—and our side should be careful to distinguish between effective defense and the use of force and provocations that end up weakening our side.

To the extent that the struggle is limited to self-appointed street fighters, it discourages mass participation, an essential condition of our success. Successful confrontations will require larger forces and higher levels of planning and organization linked closely to much more substantial mobilizations.

The experience of Boston and the Bay Area show that we should be building the largest possible united front mobilizations that bring together students, workers, unions, anti-racist organizations, women's organizations and more—to challenge the fascists, outnumber them and drive them away.

This requires us doing a number of things. First, it requires systematic propaganda that exposes the "alt-right" white nationalists for who they really are and what they really stand for. (In the meantime, they will, unfortunately, also expose themselves with their violent acts, as they did in Charlottesville.)

Second, it requires being prepared and organized to defend our side against the violence of the far right.

Third, it requires building a political alternative that links the struggles of the oppressed with struggles of ordinary workers for economic justice and unites all the forces that stand to lose from the success of the far right—which is the vast majority of working-class, young and oppressed people in the United States.

Only in this way will we be able to create the conditions in which we can effectively defeat the fascists.

The Left Is Aimless and in Need of a New, More Assertive Direction

Michael Winship

Michael Winship is the Emmy Award-winning senior writer of Moyers & Company *and BillMoyers.com, and a former senior writing fellow at the policy and advocacy group Demos.*

That's a pretty pathetic knight up there on the cover of the March issue of *Harper's Magazine*. Battered and defeated, his shield in pieces, he's slumped and saddled backwards on a Democratic donkey that has a distinctly woeful—or bored, maybe—countenance. It's the magazine's sardonic way of illustrating a powerful throwing down of the gauntlet by political scientist Adolph Reed, Jr. He has challenged the nation's progressives with an article in the magazine provocatively titled "Nothing Left: The Long, Slow Surrender of American Liberals."

His thesis flies in the face of a current spate of articles and op-ed columns touting a resurgence of progressive politics within the Democratic Party—often pointing to last year's elections of Senator Elizabeth Warren in Massachusetts and Bill de Blasio as mayor of New York City as evidence—although at the same time many of the pieces note that the wave is smashing up against a wall of resistance from the corporate wing of the party.

In a story titled, "Democrats will dive left in 2016 to distance themselves from Obama"—a headline designed to roil Republican fervor as well as impugn the opposition—the conservative *Washington Times* quoted Adam Green, cofounder of the Progressive Change Campaign Committee: "Democrats would be smart in the primary and general election to be more populist and stand up for the little guy more on economic issues."

"Liberals Face a Hard Day's Knight?" by Michael Winship, Public Square Media, Inc. This post was first published on BillMoyers.com on Feb. 25, 2014 (http://billmoyers.com/2014/02/25/liberals-face-a-hard-day%E2%80%99s-knight).

In November, Harold Meyerson wrote in the progressive magazine, *The American Prospect*, "The constituencies now swelling the Democrats' ranks, Latinos and millennials in particular, have created the space—indeed, the necessity—for the party to move to the left." And Dan Balz and Philip Rucker reported in *The Washington Post* earlier this month. "By many measures, the party is certainly seen as more liberal than it once was. For the past 40 years, the American National Election Studies surveys have asked people for their perceptions of the two major parties. The 2012 survey found, for the first time, that a majority of Americans describe the Democratic Party as liberal, with 57 percent using that label. Four years earlier, only 48 percent described the Democrats as liberal…

"Gallup reported last month that 43 percent of surveyed Democrats identified themselves as liberal, the high water mark for the party on that measurement. In Gallup's 2000 measures, just 29 percent of Democrats labeled themselves as liberals."

Nonetheless, Adolph Reed, Jr., who teaches political science at the University of Pennsylvania and is a long-time student of these things, makes a compelling case that we're hearing a death rattle more than a trumpeting call to arms.

In his *Harper*'s piece, Reed argues that Democrats and liberals have become too fixated on election results, kowtowing to the status quo rather than aiming for long term goals that address the issues of economic inequality. "…During the 1980s and early 1990s, fears of a relentless Republican juggernaut pressured those left of center to take a defensive stance," he writes, "focusing on the immediate goal of electing Democrats to stem or slow the rightward tide… Each election now becomes a moment of life-or-death urgency that precludes dissent or even reflection."

Reed says that the presidencies of Democrats Bill Clinton and Barack Obama too often acquiesced to the demands of Wall Street and the right. Of Clinton's White House years, he claims, "It is difficult to imagine that a Republican administration could have been much more successful in advancing Reaganism's agenda." And President Obama "has always been no more than an unexceptional neo-liberal Democrat with an exceptional knack for self-presentation persuasive to those who want to believe, and with solid connections and considerable good will from the corporate and financial sectors … his appeal has always been about the persona he projects—the extent to which he encourages people to feel good about their politics, the political future, and themselves through feeling good about him—than about any concrete vision or political program he has advanced. And that persona has always been bound up in and continues to play off complex and contradictory representations of race in American politics."

"The left has no particular place it wants to go," Reed asserts. "And, to rehash an old quip, if you have no destination, any direction can seem as good as any other … the left operates with no learning curve and is therefore always vulnerable to the new enthusiasm. It long ago lost the ability to move forward under its own steam…"

He continues, "With the two parties converging in policy, the areas of fundamental disagreement that separate them become too arcane and too remote from most people's experience to inspire any commitment, much less popular action. Strategies and allegiances become mercurial and opportunistic, and politics becomes ever more candidate-centered and driven by worshipful exuberance about individuals or, more accurately, the idealized and evanescent personae—the political holograms—their packagers project."

Reed concludes, "The crucial tasks for a committed left in the United States now are to admit that no politically effective force exists and to begin trying to create one. This is a long-term effort, and one that requires grounding in a vibrant labor movement. Labor may be weak or in decline, but that means aiding in its rebuilding is the most serious task for the American left. Pretending some other option exists is worse than useless."

To Accuse Antifa of Opposing Free Speech Is to Entirely Miss the Point

William Gillis

William Gillis is director of the Center for a Stateless Society (C4SS). He is also a writer and anarchist activist.

Anarchists have always paid a lot of attention to feedback loops. Seemingly small actions, small arrangements, small evils tolerated, can rapidly or inexorably build up to systematic and seemingly omnipotent power relations. Things that, in isolation don't seem that bad, can lead to the formation of states or make those states even more authoritarian. Certain economic arrangements can lead to wealth progressively concentrating power into the hands of a few. As anarchists we are always laser focused on the the dangers of letting anyone get a monopoly in anything. On the dangers of even the tiniest interpersonal acts of domination. And as radicals we never settle for established conventions, we're always questioning where what is considered "common sense" breaks down. We are always searching for the boundary conditions beyond which a rule of thumb is no longer useful. In what contexts do some dangers overwhelm other dangers?

The ideal of free speech—or as I think it should be better parsed, *freedom of information*—is an ideal of incredible importance that extends well beyond merely opposing state censorship. It's deeply worrying to see that value erode with the rhetorical ratchet of online conflict. However, freedom of speech is not as clear-cut of an ideal as some think; its application or pursuit is unavoidably tangled, as its most studied champions admit. A world of vibrant open communication where the most accurate ideas rise to the top is a *goal*—not something that can be achieved by codifying a few simplistic rules of action.

"Antifa Activists as the Truest Defenders of Free Speech," by William Gillis, The Center for a Stateless Society (C4SS), November 19, 2017.

We can all agree that cutting the telegraph wires of fascist generals coordinating an invasion would violate their personal "free speech" but it is also an action clearly justified insofar as it saves the free speech of the millions they plan to subjugate. To truly defend free speech on the whole we must sometimes deny it to its murderous enemies. To defend the ideal of a richly interconnected world where information flows freely takes more than speech, it requires action against those brutally organizing against it.

It is precisely my openness to contrary or extreme ideas, my diligence in listening to all parties, that has led me to realize complexities to free speech. In particular to recognize very extreme situations where the danger of backsliding on broadly tolerant social norms is outweighed by the danger of those ideologically committed to domination and whose recruitment proceeds not through reason but shows of force. There are always exceptions to otherwise good strategies and heuristics—as anarchists we do not rely upon the state or its obtuse and dangerous legal system and thus it is our duty as individuals to not hide from such complications. It is our responsibility as individuals to sometimes judge and act in ways that we would never trust any monopolistic institution to judge or act. Although, of course we must be careful and vigilant nonetheless.

While I inevitably have some disagreements with some among the vast and diverse array of activists who work as antifascists, I value the work that antifa groups and organizations have long undertaken to safeguard our world from the worst possible horrors. When in my neighborhood a decade ago swastikas were going up, businesses owned by people of color were being attacked, and neonazis were brutally jumping people, I certainly wasn't going to go to the police. I'm an anarchist and consistent in my opposition to the authoritarianism of the police state. But also Portland's Police—like many other departments—are themselves infested with white nationalists and broadly sympathetic to such scum. Instead I forwarded descriptions to some community members who'd gotten fed up and formed an antifa group and were actively researching and exposing these neonazis. Their work as journalists and as activists to organize boycotts and physically resist attacks helped save my neighborhood and I will never forget that. Similarly to how the faith leaders at Charlottesville attacked by neonazis will never forget the black bloc anarchists who rushed to put their bodies on the line to save their lives. As an anarchist—and the overwhelming majority of "antifa" are also diligent anarchists who reject the state as an ethical means—I've remained in the same circles and listened to what they've had to say over the years as I've traveled from city to city, country to country. I've remained consistently impressed by their scholarship, consideration, and bravery.

As full-blown fascist and white nationalist groups have recently started using the political rise of Donald Trump to infiltrate conservative protests or activism, the situation has grown more complex. And it has also become more fraught as "antifa" has suddenly entered the popular lexicon, almost warped beyond recognition. The overly-nuanced research nerds living in praiseless obscurity that I knew have abruptly been cast as violence worshipping thugs, or frothing naive college kids looking to punch anyone problematic. This is, as all anarchists know, absolutely incorrect, although such cartoonish and disconnected narratives clearly further the agendas of both liberals and conservatives. Sadly, in some respects this media narrative becoming a self-fulfilling prophesy that marginalizes longstanding antifa groups, and casts things into much broader conflict of Trump supporters (as "nazis") versus any and all Trump opponents (as "antifa"), an astonishingly ignorant framing that only benefits fascist entryists and helps spread misinformation via mainstream partisan paranoia.

But there clearly are important ethical and strategic challenges that the mainstream analysis among antifascist activists presents to the rest of us.

- When nazis hold a march with guns through a jewish neighborhood is that really just a matter of open discourse?
- Where does a reasonable boundary of "imminence" or "likelihood" to a threat get drawn?

- How many people need to be killed and at what frequency for us to see ourselves as at war?
- If a group organizes so that one wing works as streetfighters and murderers and another wing as public spokesmen and recruiters should we really be obligated to treat them as distinct groups or at what point should we see them as the same entity?

Many of these questions would be revolting if it was the leviathan state itself we were trusting to judge such distinctions. But we are anarchists, and as autonomous individuals our ethical responsibilities and capacities are different. Where institutions may have to behave as *rule consequentialists* lest their bureaucratic momentum carry them to terrible places, individual minds have the agency—and responsibility—to often behave more as *act consequentialists*, capable of recognizing nuance and context in ways that are more finely grained. Rather than sticking with hamfisted rules we can examine the specific context of each possible action before us.

I agree with the dominant antifascist critique of liberalism and its shortsightedness. Liberals do not grasp the threat posed by fascism—they over-privilege the perceived stability of their institutions and the status quo. They codify simplistic codes of behavior modeled upon the state's legal system—and naturally, the fascists can run rings around these. Liberals happily legitimize fascists through debate, failing to realize that the game fascists are playing isn't the game of reason, but the game of psychological appeals. As a practical matter fascism succeeds in debate—in the sense of quickly mobilizing enough of the population to achieve its aims—because the truth is complex, whereas false but simplistic narratives are often more emotionally resonant.

[…]

In Defense of Antifascist Activism

For decades antifa have served a niche role as watchmen, as relatively lonely nazi hunters and researchers. Their ranks would occasionally swell when a particularly noticeable infection of fascists cropped up, as local community members would step up to join in resisting them. But what has happened in the last two years is utterly off the scale.

It's a little stunning to be an anarchist in this context. It's like watching an impassioned national conversation about Food Not Bombs or Anarchist Black Cross. A longtime staple of the anarchist movement, a franchised friendly neighborhood project the rest of us don't think about much, has been weirdly thrust into the spotlight. Literally everyone is scrambling to identify with it or against it, and to redefine it into their personal political narratives.

Trump is both central to this recent story and at the same time almost entirely vestigial. He's a reflexively authoritarian political figure who has aptly played to the nativist and racist tendencies in his reactionary base far more explicitly than arguably even Nixon, but he's also an idiot opportunistic figurehead being used and bounced between different forces. While Trump himself will do some immense amount of damage—like all Presidents—the unique dangers of his presidency are that he'll serve as a catalyst to fascist and reactionary forces. Will he effectively unleash the police and set off this century's Palmer raids of dissidents? Will he institute mass deportations and ethnic cleansing? F*ck it, will he start a war that kills tens of millions? These questions hang in the air every day. They are important and pressing and we must be ready to resist them but, *policy* is not a traditional concern of antifascists. There's already an array of activist institutions in some sense prepared to deal with these potential atrocities. In contrast, what antifascists have focused on is fascist organizing. In keeping the seemingly marginal nuts, marginal.

Now the wall keeping explicit fascists out of society has mostly come down and no one knows what comes next.

While antifascists are adapting and innovating, so far they have responded mostly by escalating their traditional means of reporting, doxing, and physically disrupting fascist organizing. This laser focus has its benefits, but it just as clearly has its downsides. Antifascist groups were formed to organize community self defense against nazis, not to win a media battle in the mainstream. Their skillset is investigative reporting, organizing and physical resistance, not media narrative crafting. As a result they were obviously completely unprepared to counter the abrupt mainstreaming of fascism into the public discourse, handle the rapid rise in people identifying as "antifa," or counter narratives painting antifa as somehow bad.

At the root of the bad press antifa has been getting and the success of reactionaries in spreading lies about them is a tension over "media relations" and public outreach that anarchists have felt for ages.

> Worrying about whether we're giving them material for their lies is a fool's neuroticism. They're going to make up fake news anyway—turning a fascist who lost a fight into an innocent bystander or lending credence to the guy who stabbed himself and blamed antifa. The truth is that most pundits (on the right and supposed left) are happy to fall for these "vicious antifa" stories because these pundits are more concerned with order than justice. For them, people fighting in the street over politics will always conjure images of other countries where they don't want to live. It upsets them.[1]

Your reaction to this will depend in no small part on whether you think the war for public opinion is critical or centrally important to the struggle against fascism. I think the real challenge of the Trump era is that the public opinion and media narrative game HAS started to matter in a way that wasn't previously true when it came to antifascist activism. But I'm not convinced that public opinion or media narratives are of such importance as to eclipse all other issues. I think it's worth critically evaluating that assumption. Most Americans grow up indoctrinated in the assumptions of liberal democracy, shaping our every instinct to think that winning public opinion or "a majority" is the *definition* of success. There's often a lot of baggage preventing people from evaluating or really thinking in terms of direct action—of just getting a thing done, regardless of whether you're widely hated for doing it. Running the underground railroad in the antebellum south was not remotely about winning hearts and minds among the white population—it was about immediately freeing slaves. Going against the wishes of the majority not to eventually persuade them, but to directly impede their capacity to oppress is often a quite valid means. We would today rightfully scoff at those condemning the underground railroad for "undermining the struggle for public opinion" by breaking the law and thus contributing to white fears. And we could spin a similar analogy here when it came to vigilante violence against slave owners.

It's important to remember that antifascist groups exist in large part because anarchists don't trust the state to respond to white supremacists (and Islamists like ISIS), and want to disrupt the organizing of such would-be-tyrants without appealing to the state's cancerous monopoly on violence. Much of the historic squabbling between antifascists and liberal groups like the Southern Poverty Law Center has centered around precisely whether the state can be trusted with "hate crimes" laws or "anti-extremism" efforts.

I keep saying "anarchist" because let's be honest—despite there being liberal, socialist, and libertarian members of antifa groups, antifascism has been predominately an anarchist project since the end of the second world war, championed and directed by anarchists. Especially in the United States where antifascism is overwhelmingly an anarchist project. Antifascist work is necessarily done in secret with no reward of social capital and no hierarchical machinery to seize, and thus has been of little interest to statist communists who prefer infiltrating and seizing control over liberal organizations.

Of course antifa is varied, active for decades across numerous countries, in a variety of contexts. The European model is more broad subcultural and marxist-influenced, the American model both more tightly organized and anarchist. But differences abound between regions and countries. And antifa groups or campaigns often emerge in ways specific to subcultures and scenes. Fascists have consistently tried to build subcultural bases by infiltrating and corrupting existing ones, and so you get people in skinhead, punk, goth, metal, paganism, libertarianism, etc, exposing and pushing back against them. Naturally these antifa all look different and take different approaches. But if there's universal conclusions one can extract it's that it's worth being hated if you're also able to rally people to expel a popular band or figure, and that in many circumstances only a willingness to use physical force will get the job done.

[…]

Notes

1. Harris, Malcolm. "Why the Media Refuses to Understand Antifa." Pacific Standard, August 31, 2017, https://psmag.com/social-justice/understanding-antifa.

History and Social Science Are Not on Antifa's Side

Molly Wallace

Molly Wallace is a contributing editor at the Peace Science Digest *and a visiting scholar in Portland State University's Conflict Resolution Program. Her new book,* Security Without Weapons: Rethinking Violence, Nonviolent Action, and Civilian Protection, *explores nonviolent alternatives for civilian protection in war zones.*

W e've all heard the argument before: However "nice" the use of nonviolence may be, in the real world violence is necessary—and ultimately more effective, so the thinking goes—for challenging a brutal regime, fighting injustice or defending against an armed opponent. But what are the actual effects of adding violence to a movement's repertoire of resistance strategies?

Previous scholarship has been inconclusive on this question of so-called "radical flank effects," as studies tend to focus on individual cases and also reflect collective confusion over what is meant by "radical." Does it, for instance, refer to the means used or the ends sought?

Focusing, therefore, on violent—as opposed to "radical"—flanks, researchers Erica Chenoweth and Kurt Schock sought to bring clarity and systematic analysis to bear on this question of positive versus negative violent flank effects. In a 2015 article for the journal Mobilization, they examined all nonviolent campaigns from 1900-2006 with radical (i.e. "maximalist") goals—such as the "removal of an incumbent national government, self-determination, secession, or the expulsion of foreign occupation"—to see how the presence or absence of armed resistance affected the success of these nonviolent campaigns. Their findings offer compelling

---

"The strategic Naiveté of Antifa," by Molly Wallace, originally published by Waging Nonviolence, January 4, 2018. Reprinted by permission.

evidence that violence is not generally a helpful addition to nonviolent resistance movements.

How did they arrive at this conclusion? Using both quantitative and qualitative research methods, the authors begin by generating three hypotheses. First, nonviolent campaigns with violent flanks are more likely to succeed than nonviolent campaigns without violent flanks. Second, nonviolent campaigns without violent flanks are more likely to succeed than nonviolent campaigns with violent flanks. And third, violent flanks have no impact on the success rates of nonviolent campaigns.

To test these hypotheses, they search for any significant statistical relationships that might exist between the presence of violent flanks and the success or failure of nonviolent campaigns. They find none, thus providing no support for either the first or second hypothesis. As the authors note, this could mean either that the presence of violent flanks has no discernible effect on outcomes or that it has mixed positive and negative effects that cancel each other out when taken together.

When they compare the effects of violent flanks that emerge from inside a nonviolent movement to those of violent flanks that develop parallel to a nonviolent movement, they find that the former are associated with failure, suggesting that negative violent flank effects are more pronounced when a nonviolent campaign cannot distance itself from its armed counterpart. Moreover, they find that mass participation is the strongest determinant of nonviolent campaign success and that the presence of violent flanks has a negative effect on participation levels, suggesting that violent flanks may indirectly decrease the likelihood of success.

To flesh out how violent flanks operate within individual cases, Chenoweth and Schock examine four cases where violent flanks were present: Burma in 1988, the Philippines from 1983-1986, South Africa from 1952-1961 and South Africa from 1983-1994. Two campaigns were successful (the Philippines and South Africa from 1983-1994) and two were not (Burma and South Africa from 1952-1961). Meanwhile, two had violent flanks outside of the nonviolent movement (Burma and the Philippines) and two had violent flanks associated with the nonviolent movement (the two South Africa cases).

After examining the histories of these nonviolent campaigns—and the ways they interacted with armed resistance—the authors find mixed results. Violent flanks had negative effects in the two unsuccessful cases, no net impact in one of the successful cases (the Philippines) and a weak positive effect in the other (the later South African case). Overall there was greater evidence for negative violent flank effect mechanisms than for positive ones.

In the one case where a violent flank had a weak positive effect (South Africa from 1983-1994), Chenoweth and Schock argue that that effect was mostly symbolic—energizing activists around the revolutionary mystique of violent resistance—rather than instrumental to gaining power over the apartheid regime (something that was accomplished, instead, by the nonviolent resistance movement).

However, in the two cases where violent flanks had negative effects, these effects were seriously detrimental. The presence of an armed movement, according to the authors, diminished "chances of success for otherwise nonviolent campaigns by legitimating repression, demobilizing participants, shifting to violent strategies where the state [wa]s superior, and discrediting regime opponents."

Notably, the armed movements were consistently shown not to protect nonviolent activists but rather to put them at greater risk, as authorities used the presence of armed actors to justify widespread repression against all resistance movements, violent and nonviolent alike.

Chenoweth and Schock find evidence in the case studies, then, that violent flanks do actually influence the outcomes of nonviolent campaigns, despite the earlier quantitative findings suggesting otherwise. Negative and positive effects simply appear to cancel each other out when taken together over a large number of cases, with negative violent flank effects being somewhat more prominent than positive ones. The authors argue, therefore, that "on average, maximalist nonviolent campaigns often succeed *despite* violent flanks—rarely because of them."

Contemporary Relevance

Despite recent scholarship demonstrating the greater effectiveness of nonviolent resistance (see Erica Chenoweth and Maria Stephan's 2011 book, "Why Civil Resistance Works"), assumptions about the effectiveness of violence—along with its supposedly radical and/ or revolutionary nature—stubbornly persist. When faced with a brutal or blatantly unjust opponent, many people are inclined to believe that only violence will bring about needed change or be able to protect and defend one's community or fellow activists.

We have seen this recent thinking everywhere from Syria to Venezuela, but for those of us in the United States struggling against the Trump administration and the white supremacist and neo-Nazi forces it has unleashed, we need look no further than the presence of Antifa (anti-fascist groups who do not rule out engaging in violent confrontations) in our own protests to see this same logic at work—as well as its counterproductive effects. Such groups see themselves as a necessary counterpart to white supremacist or neo-Nazi groups who come armed to demonstrations, ready to engage in street battles with left-wing activists.

Although this logic of needing to use violence to defend against violence is so widespread and deeply ingrained as to be almost intuitive, the problem is that such moves feed into and reinforce narratives on the right that inspire—and provide cover for—their own claims to self-defense. Just as the presence of a violent flank in an anti-regime nonviolent movement can provide necessary or further justification for government security forces to fire on protesters, so too can it create a similar dynamic among non-state groups, including neo-Nazis and white supremacists, mobilizing more recruits and ultimately increasing the vulnerability of anti-racist and anti-fascist activists and the marginalized and targeted communities whom they wish to defend.

Practical Implications

In the wake of recent events in Charlottesville, outrage has rightly focused on the neo-Nazi and white supremacist groups who came armed and even killed one of the counter-protesters. Their goals of racial supremacy and purity, fueled by hate and fear and devoid of empathy, have no place in a country that values equality, pluralism and human dignity, and their ascendancy at the moment is nothing short of terrifying.

For the sake of effectively challenging these groups and their repulsive vision, however, those of us who consider ourselves part of the resistance must also engage in critical inward reflection, especially with regards to the strategic implications of the presence of Antifa affiliates who also came armed to Charlottesville, among otherwise nonviolent counter-protesters.

Although their work to expose and tirelessly organize against fascism is admirable and necessary, those who identify with Antifa and its full range of tactics appear to endorse at least two flawed assumptions. First, they assume that truly radical action to effectively challenge fascism must include violence—what is often termed "physical confrontation"—and that nonviolence equals "dialogue" or "normal politics," which implies acquiescence, submission or cooptation. Second, they assume that violence is also necessary to protect activists and targeted communities.

But, in fact, here is what we know from recent social scientific research: Nonviolent resistance is twice as likely to be effective as violent resistance when used for radical goals such as the removal of an authoritarian regime or national liberation, cases with no shortage of brutal, unreasonable opponents. Furthermore, nonviolent resistance strategy is all about analyzing and dismantling an opponent's sources of power, including through direct action. Finally, as noted in Chenoweth and Schock's research above, instead of protecting nonviolent activists, the presence of a violent flank frequently creates justification for *further* repression against them, making them *more* vulnerable to violence.

It is time, therefore, that we untether violence from its "radical" and "protective/defensive" associations. Not doing so—and hanging on, as Antifa does, to these tired old assertions that violence is a necessary response—is, quite simply, poor strategy. It gives white supremacists and neo-Nazis exactly what they want, reinforcing their "we're embattled" narratives, thereby strengthening their movement. It muddies the waters by giving commentators on the right something to point to when they try to create ludicrous moral equivalencies between white supremacists/neo-Nazis and anti-fascist activists. And, in doing so, it does nothing to actually diminish the strength of white supremacism.

Furthermore, the continued presence of armed elements like Antifa has negative effects within the resistance. Speaking from personal experience, as the mother of a three-year-old, it makes me, for one, feel more vulnerable to violence and therefore less likely to show up to demonstrations with my daughter. I can only assume that many others—not just parents—feel and act similarly, resulting in diminished mass participation in the movement and thereby a decrease in its power and effectiveness.

For all these reasons, if Antifa activists care—as they no doubt do—about challenging resurgent fascist, white supremacist forces effectively, they must think more strategically, considering the short- and long-term effects of their actions. Although "punching a Nazi" may feel like effective action due to the immediate, physical consequences of violence—someone's bloody nose, someone's body on the ground—what actually matters for the strategic value of an action is how others respond to it afterwards.

Does it strengthen the opponent group—reinforcing its narratives, drawing more recruits and unifying them against a more easily vilified adversary—or weaken it? Does it strengthen one's own side—drawing a broader array of activists of all ages and from all walks of life to the resistance movement, unified around a common vision—or weaken it? Does it bring uncommitted third parties to one's side or alienate them? These—not the number of individuals punched or bludgeoned on the other side—should be the metrics of a strategic response to fascism.

The dangers of white supremacism and fascism are real, and the stakes for American democracy and values are high. It is precisely for these reasons that activists need to engage in discussions about the strategic merits and radical credentials of disciplined nonviolent resistance (both for movement effectiveness and for protection), together strategizing about those actions that will best diminish the power of the opponent to realize its white supremacist, fascist agenda. A few points, in particular, are worth raising.

First, despite common-sense associations of violent action with defense and protection, nonviolent discipline has a better chance of keeping activists safe than armed resistance does, even—counter-intuitively—in the face of a violent adversary. There is no guarantee of complete safety with either type of resistance, but armed resistance is much more likely to elicit further—not less—violence from the other side.

Nonetheless, assumptions about arms and their role in defense or protection are so engrained that this is a tough point to get across. If presented with a scenario where a few unarmed activists in a completely nonviolent movement are killed by armed opponents versus one where a greater number of unarmed activists are killed by these opponents while joined by fellow armed activists fighting back, most of us are likely to characterize the unarmed activists in the first instance as "defenseless" and those in the second instance as being "defended," despite the fact that they were, in fact, better protected in the first instance. These deeply engrained—and flawed—assumptions about the defensive or protective value of weapons must be brought to the surface and critically examined.

Second, there is a strategic logic to nonviolent resistance that most Antifa adherents seem to not know (as demonstrated through the claim on one Antifa website that "only popular self-defense, not simply debate, has succeeded in stopping fascism" or statements made by various Antifa activists in the *New York Times* suggesting that our choice in response to fascism takes binary form: use violence or "do nothing").

Far from being synonymous with "debate" or inaction, nonviolent resistance involves the dismantling of an opponent's sources of power through a range of methods, including various forms of disruption and direct action, and is twice as likely as violent resistance to succeed in achieving radical goals. In other words, the success of nonviolent resistance does not depend on the presence—and persuasion—of a "nice" adversary.

Contrary to mainstream belief, there is a historical record of successful nonviolent resistance against fascism in countries under Nazi control, including the Rosenstrasse demonstrations in Berlin where wives saved their Jewish husbands, Denmark's rescue of most of its Jewish community, resistance to the Nazi policies of the Quisling government in Norway, and so on. Jacques Semelin's 1993 book "Unarmed Against Hitler" is one resource that examines these and other cases throughout Europe.

Third, only by maintaining nonviolent discipline can the resistance dramatize and capitalize on the clear contrast between its activists and the white supremacists or neo-Nazis they confront. Stooping to the level of armed hooligans on the other side, engaging them on their own terms, weakens the anti-fascist cause by surrendering the high ground in media representations of demonstrations, providing cover for commentators who wish to draw a specious moral equivalency between the two sides, and alienating people who would otherwise ally themselves with an anti-fascist movement.

Finally, violence is less—not more—"radical" than nonviolence is, especially insofar as it is less effective in achieving radical goals and less likely to dismantle white supremacism and fascism than nonviolent resistance. Far from embodying a radical challenge to fascism, Antifa affiliates are doing exactly what neo-Nazis and white supremacists are hoping they will do—this is precisely the reaction that will energize the very fascists they are hoping to shut down, reinforcing their embattled narratives and strengthening their ranks.

Only by disassociating one's radical credentials from participation in violence will we ultimately move away from these knee-jerk responses to racist violence that do nothing to minimize the draw and strength of white supremacy—and instead move towards more strategic, effective action that actually has a chance of advancing the cause of a diverse, inclusive, just society.

Antifa's Tactics Play Directly into the Hands of Right Wing Ideologues

Joshua M. Patton

Joshua M. Patton is a freelance writer and researcher. His writing focuses on news, politics, entertainment, and culture.

I n recent weeks, there has been a lot of attention paid, particularly on the right, to the masked, typically black-clad anarchist protesters who go by the name "Antifa," mobilizing as a political group on the left that is not afraid to use violence. Their stated motivation is to prevent the United States from descending into an authoritarian nightmare, but what they don't seem to realize is that they are the key to it happening.

It should be stated from the outset that efforts to directly compare Antifa and far-right extremist groups are either woefully misguided or deliberate false equivalence. The data clearly show[1] that in the United States more people have been killed since September 11, 2001 by far-right terrorists[2] than any other group. In 2002 testimony from Congress from Dale L. Watson[3], then one of the leads in the Counterrorism Division of the bureau, warned of the threat of white supremacist terror. The DHS and the FBI sent a report to the Trump Administration in May[4] (dated one day after former Director James Comey's impromptu firing) warning about the threat of white supremacists. Heather Heyer was the latest victim of this violence, when a Nazi fanatic mowed down protesters in Charlottesville, Virginia in August.[5]

So, while Antifa represents a meager and pathetic "terror threat" by comparison, the group's success in the Trump Era is a cause for concern, both because of what it means about the fringe of the left in the US and how Antifa's actions may bring about the exact sort of fascist dystopia they claim to wish to prevent.

"How Antifa Is the Trump Administration's Best Friend," by Joshua M. Patton, Medium, September 5, 2017. Reprinted by permission of the author.

Antifa caught the attention of the FBI in early 2015, according to reporting by Politico,[6] after the Trump campaign really started to pick up steam and stoke the nativist tensions in the GOP primary voters of the American heartland. The bureau called their activities "domestic terrorist violence," though this does not mean that Antifa itself has been labeled a terror group. (Nor should it be, but more on that later.)

Now, as we get into the final fourth of Trump's first year as president, Antifa has mobilized in cities from coast to coast[7] to shut down events featuring right-wing speakers, from overt white supremacists to media vultures like Ann Coulter who cater to them. Defenders of Antifa see this as a victory, especially those engagements that were shut down simply because of the threat of violence, such as the Portland Rose Parade.[8] (Which, arguably, had exactly nothing to do with fascism.)

When they don't shut down the event beforehand, things get bloody. In Berkeley, California last week black-clad Antifa members attacked Trump supporters[9] when both groups showed up for competing rallies at Martin Luther King Jr. Civic Center Park. That the assault of the peaceful Trump supporters (and the majority of the "Rally Against Hate" protesters were also peaceful) happened in a park named after America's purest historical representative of nonviolent civil disobedience is the insult to this political injury.

Of course, Antifa has its own historical roots that date back to Europe in advance of the second World War. At the time in Germany the political opponents of the Nazis were the Social Democrats and the Communists. While these were two disparate groups in terms of ideology and beliefs, they realized that they had to unite if they wanted to fight the takeover of their country. These "Antifaschistische" groups tried (and failed) to both prevent Hitler's rise to power and to fight the fascists in the streets.

After the war was over, according to an Office of Military Government report[10] covering the post-WWII decade in Europe, noted that Antifa existed after the war but, like today, they were a small and disparate collection of groups with no central ideology or leader. They focused mainly on " hunting down Nazi criminals and underground Nazi partisans (the so-called "Werewolves") and practical concerns affecting the general population," according to report from *Jacobin*.[11] Eventually the Antifa members were absorbed into the post-war political parties that arose and the group was extinct until the late 1970s.

The punk music era bucked the establishment those original Antifa members helped to build in the 30 years since the war's end. Because the movement appealed to political and social outcasts, those on the far-right and far-left found themselves rocking to the same shows. However leftists and anarchists in the Berlin punk scene[12] objected to the burgeoning neo-Nazi movement revived the violent tactics of the Antifa of the past.[13] However, instead of directing this violence towards a fascist power structure the revived Antifa were beating up sh*thead loners who needed something, anything to hate in order to make themselves feel less like sh*thead loners.

And that difference is what makes the modern Antifa so dangerous, because despite President Trump's best efforts, the United States is not an authoritarian police state. Instead, they keep attacking random citizens who have no real power. This is, unquestionably, against the law and could perhaps be used to inspire increased "protective" measures that limit key rights like freedom of expression and the right to assemble.

This sort of violence is a gift to the Trump administration who'd love nothing more than to strengthen their "law and order" bona fides by cracking down these rights in the face of this so-called "terrorist threat." They are forcing the hands of even the most liberal areas to take steps to crack down on Antifa with policies that are the proverbial "slippery slope" that would lead to more "danger." In the aftermath of the 2016 violence in Berkeley, some in state government tried to have them declared terrorists, according to *The Los Angeles Times*.[14] While that's not likely to pass, they are debating whether or not to label them a "street gang," which are subject to fewer legal protections than run-of-the-mill criminals.

It doesn't matter that the Antifa types are a loose collection of American socialists and anarchists[15] (both who feel like "burning it all down" is not a bad idea), their actions and propensity to wear a uniform aid the Trump administration in painting them as a homegrown violent movement that must be stamped out to keep everyone safe. While direct comparisons of the Trump administration and Hitler's Reich are irresponsible, there is a parallel between how left-wing violence fueled and later cemented Hitler's public support.

As Ron Grossman writes for *The Chicago Tribune:*[16]

> Germany was stripped of the military might that was its glory. With the old order in tatters, cultural freedom abounded. A new openness about sexuality was welcomed by some but considered decadent by others.
>
> To all those confused by that period of rapid change, Hitler had simple answers: Order must be restored. The Jews must be punished. A martial spirit must return. Other nations must cease disrespecting us or suffer the consequences.

In Trump's America, his supporters have suffered while wages stagnated and jobs disappeared. Conservative media tells them that everyone—gays, illegal immigrants, and minorities—are getting everything for free while they are ignored by the liberals and the Republican establishment. It's no accident that Trump saw campaign success by calling his supporters the "forgotten people"[17] and providing them with the same sort of "easy answers" that make authoritarianism feel like protection.

Donald Trump would speak to his supporters about issues using a simple three-part structure that made his "ideas" (even when factually incorrect) easy to latch on to.[18] Let's examine his infamous claim that immigrants were drug dealers and rapists, which showcases this structure nicely.

Trump starts off by calling the US a "dumping ground for everybody else's problems." He then immediately gives his audience a scapegoat for the problem, in this case it's immigrants, but he also uses Obama, Hillary Clinton, Democrats, and the media as foils also. And then his solution is simply that he's the only one who can fix it, and he can fix it "fast" (just so long as those pesky checks and balances in the government stay out of his way).

So, if Antifa keeps up their violent assaults on his supporters and random people with high-and-tight haircuts, they have become the sort of foil that will not only win him support but could be leveraged into helping him weaken the American institutions he so detests because they limit his power to act unilaterally. His supporters are already primed for it, with significant percentages of Republicans blaming immigrants[19] for their woes and believing that Whites and Christians—America's two largest demographic majorities—face discrimination.[20] A crackdown on freedoms to defend America from these left-wing "terrorists" would be greeted with, to quote *Star Wars,*[21] "thunderous applause."

It does seem odd for Americans, whose very country was born out of bloodshed and war, to object to political violence. As Thomas Jefferson famously wrote to William Smith in 1787[22] (two years before the US Constitution was ratified) "the tree of liberty must be refreshed from time to time with the blood of patriots and tyrants." (Though, it doesn't mean what most people think it means.[23]) Jefferson was being ironic, and the whole of the letter is an argument that Shay's rebellion was misguided and foolish.

However, if Antifa and those on the left who support their tactics want to say that their violence is justified to fight the oppressors they are essentially saying that it's time to shut off the lights and lock the door on that government founded in the late 18th-century by and for the people.

Like the Antifa of old, the American Revolutionaries turned to violence and rebellion only after they petitioned parliament in defense of their rights[24] and were branded traitors for it. When a group decides that it's time for politically-inspired violence, they are saying that the government is not only broken, it's not worth saving. That is a message that will be tough for Americans to get behind, even if they object to Trump.[25]

There has been a trend on the left to seemingly adopt the worst characteristics of the Tea Party,[26] specifically an aversion to compromise and an insistence on ideological "purity." However, even at their worst, the Tea Party folks never turned to violence. Instead they organized (and accepted untracked political donations) to win the House of Representatives, control of more than half of the state governments, and, in 2014, the Senate for the Republican party. They have stopped worrying about convincing those they disagree with that their point-of-view is correct or superior. And the best way to do that is through education and peaceful protest, not violent clashes with police and the public.

Because, no matter what you think, peaceful protest works. As noted, the greatest protest figure in US history was Martin Luther King Jr. who, with the help of a sympathetic president in Lyndon B. Johnson, saw his protest agenda codified into legislation. Today a huge monument to him stands in the nation's capital and his likeness sits in the Oval Office, even with Trump behind the Resolute Desk.

There is also no question that peaceful protests and engagement with elected representatives helped to defeat the GOP effort to end the Affordable Care Act and helped to (at least) weaken the "temporary" travel ban. These members of the so-called "Resistance" lobbied for their cause nonviolently (for the most part[27]) and convinced Republicans to buck their party to defeat these measures.

A study from Erica Chenoweth of the University of Denver[28] found that from 1900 to 2006, nonviolent political movements succeed a majority of the time, while more than 60 percent of violent movements fail. When there is only "limited success" nonviolent movements still double the progress made by violent movements.

Princeton University researcher Omar Wasow found in a recent study that where white voters were in close proximity to peaceful protests in the 1960s, they voted to support liberal candidates like John F. Kennedy and Johnson. However, where there were violent protests (specifically riots in the wake of King's assassination), white voters went overwhelmingly to the conservative, "law and order" candidate, in this case Richard Nixon.

While it may be a leap in probability that America will become a fascist dictatorship under President Trump, there is no question that if Antifa keeps up their violence it will definitely help likeminded GOP candidates in the 2018 midterms and help him keep the White House in 2020.

Notes

1. https://theintercept.com/2017/05/31/the-numbers-dont-lie-white-far-right-terrorists-pose-a-cleardanger-to-us-all/

2. https://www.documentcloud.org/documents/3924852-White-Supremacist-Extremism-JIB.html

3. https://archives.fbi.gov/archives/news/testimony/the-terrorist-threat-confronting-the-unitedstates

4. https://www.axios.com/fbi-and-dhs-reported-persistent-white-supremacy-threat-in-may-1513304834-8c99815f-98a7-4052-921f-a5f5b827cbc4.html

5. https://medium.com/@JoshuaMPatton/the-lesson-for-white-people-in-the-charlottesville-tragedyyes-racism-still-exists-in-america-and-a76e51792b08

6. https://www.politico.com/story/2017/09/01/antifa-charlottesville-violence-fbi-242235

7. https://www.revealnews.org/article/antifa-has-a-rapid-response-team-that-targets-alt-rightorganizers/

8. https://www.washingtonpost.com/news/morning-mix/wp/2017/04/27/portland-rose-paradecanceled-after-antifascists-threaten-gop-marchers/

9 .https://www.washingtonpost.com/news/morning-mix/wp/2017/08/28/black-clad-antifa-attackright-wing-demonstrators-in-berkeley/?utm_term=.af0b9c2d0698

10. https://books.google.co.uk/books?id=RfkqAAAAMAAJ&q="antifa"&dq="antifa"&hl=en&sa=X&ved=0ahUKEwjRvLB2O_VAhUjKMAKHVY9B7AQ6AEINDAD

11. https://www.jacobinmag.com/2017/05/antifascist-movements-hitler-nazis-kpd-spd-germanycold-war

12. https://www.washingtonpost.com/news/book-party/wp/2017/09/01/the-history-theory-andcontradictions-of-antifa/?utm_term=.0ec7dd007b4f

13. https://www.theatlantic.com/magazine/archive/2017/09/the-rise-of-the-violent-left/534192/

14. http://www.latimes.com/local/lanow/la-me-ln-antifa-gang-20170904-story.html

15. https://bpr.berkeley.edu/2017/03/23/antifa-a-new-political-resistance/

16 .http://www.chicagotribune.com/news/columnists/ct-met-grossman-column-antifa-20170829-story.html

17. https://www.usatoday.com/story/news/politics/2017/01/20/donald-trump-inauguration-daypresident-white-house/96782700/

18. https://www.youtube.com/watch?v=_aFo_BV-UzI

19 https://latest.com/2016/05/two-charts-can-explain-why-trump-has-been-so-successful-withrepublican-voters/

20. https://latest.com/2017/02/data-shows-trump-supporters-white-victimhood-panic-makes-themthe-real-snowflakes/
21. https://www.youtube.com/watch?v=DgxZr6LLS34
22. http://wiki.monticello.org/mediawiki/index.php/The_tree_of_liberty...%28Quotation%29
23. https://latest.com/2016/08/the-2nd-amendment-does-not-exist-to-fight-tyranny-though-it-canhelp/
24. http://www.loc.gov/teachers/classroommaterials/presentationsandactivities/presentations/timeline/amrev/rebelln/rights.html
25. http://nypost.com/2017/09/04/nancy-pelosi-stands-up-for-civilization-against-antifa/
26. https://latest.com/2016/07/day-1-of-dnc-shows-that-the-progressive-left-is-becoming-like-thetea-party/
27. https://www.youtube.com/watch?v=HLPOIgnp6WE
28. https://www.washingtonpost.com/news/worldviews/wp/2013/11/05/peaceful-protest-is-muchmore-effective-than-violence-in-toppling-dictators/

Antifa-Style Activism Will Not Stop the Wave of Reactionary Populism Currently Sweeping the Globe

Slavoj Žižek

Slavoj Žižek is a Slovenian philosopher and cultural critic. He is a professor at the European Graduate School, International Director of the Birkbeck Institute for the Humanities, Birkbeck College, University of London, and a senior researcher at the Institute of Sociology, University of Ljubljana, Slovenia. His books include Living in the End Times, First as Tragedy, Then as Farce, *and* In Defense of Lost Causes.

Marx's formula of religion as the opium of the people needs some serious rethinking today. It is true that radical Islam is an exemplary case of religion as the opium of the people: a false confrontation with capitalist modernity which allows some fundamentalist Muslims to dwell in their ideological dream while their countries are ravaged by the effects of global capitalism—and exactly the same holds for Christian fundamentalism. However, there are today, in our Western world, two other versions of the opium of the people: the opium and the people.

As Laurent de Sutter demonstrated, chemistry (in its scientific version) is becoming part of us: large aspects of our lives are characterised by the management of our emotions by drugs, from everyday use of sleeping pills and antidepressants to hard narcotics. We are not just controlled by impenetrable social powers; our very emotions are "outsourced" to chemical stimulation.

The stakes of this chemical intervention are double and contradictory: we use drugs to keep external excitement (shocks, anxieties and so on) under control, i.e., to desensitise us for them,

"Today's Anti-fascist Movement Will Do Nothing to Get Rid of Right-Wing Populism–It's Just Panicky Posturing," by Slavoj Žižek, *The Independent*, December 7, 2017. Reprinted by permission.

and to generate artificial excitement if we are depressed and lack desire.

As the rise of populism demonstrates, the opium of the people is "the people" itself, the fuzzy populist dream destined to obfuscate our own antagonisms. However, I want to add to this series: anti-fascism itself.

A new spectre is haunting progressive politics in Europe and the US, the spectre of fascism. Trump in the US, le Pen in France, Orban in Hungary—they are all demonised as the new evil towards which we should unite all our force. Every minimal doubt and reserve is immediately proclaimed a sign of secret collaboration with fascism.

In a remarkable interview for *Der Spiegel* published in October 2017, Emmanuel Macron made some statements received enthusiastically by all who want to fight the new fascist right: "There are three possible ways to react to right-wing extremist parties. The first is to act as though they don't exist and to no longer risk taking political initiatives that could get these parties against you. That has happened many times in France and we have seen that it doesn›t work. The people who you are actually hoping to support no longer see themselves reflected in your party›s speeches. And it allows the right wing to build its audience.

"The second reaction is to chase after these right-wing extremist parties in fascination … and the third possibility is to say, these people are my true enemies and to engage them in battle. Exactly that is the story of the second round of the presidential election in France."

While Macron's stance is commendable, it is crucial to supplement it by a self-critical turn. The demonised image of a fascist threat clearly serves as a new political fetish, fetish in the simple Freudian sense of a fascinating image whose function is to obfuscate the true antagonism.

Fascism itself is immanently fetishist: it needs a figure like that of a Jew, elevated into the external cause of our troubles—such a figure enables us to obfuscate the real antagonisms which cut across our societies.

Exactly the same holds for the figure of "fascist" in today's liberal imagination: it enables people to obfuscate deadlocks which lie at the root of our crisis.

When, in the last elections in France, every leftist scepticism about Macron was immediately denounced as a support for le Pen, the elimination of the left was the true aim of the operation, and the demonised enemy was a convenient prop to sustain this elimination.

The fear not to make any compromises with the alt-right can muddy the degree to which we are already compromised by it. One should greet every sign of this self-critical reflection which is gradually emerging and which, while remaining thoroughly anti-fascist, casts also a critical glance on the weaknesses of the liberal left.

When I drew attention to how parts of the alt-right are mobilising working class issues neglected by the liberal left, I was, as expected, immediately accused of pleading for a coalition between radical left and fascist right, which is exactly what I didn't propose. The task is to cut off the working class oxygen supply to the alt-right by addressing their voter. The way to achieve this is to move more to the left with a more radical critical message—in other words, to do exactly what Sanders and Corbyn were doing and what was the root of their relative success.

The same goes for the topic of refugees. Refugees mostly don't want to live in Europe; they want a decent life back at home. Instead of working to achieve that, Western powers treat the problem as a "humanitarian crisis" whose two extremes are hospitality and the fear of losing our way of life. They thereby create a pseudo-"cultural" conflict between refugees and local working class populations, engaging them in a false conflict which transforms a political and economic struggle into one of the "clash of civilisations."

The sad prospect that awaits us is that of a future in which, every four years, we will be thrown into a panic, scared by some form of "neo-fascist danger," and in this way blackmailed into casting our vote for the "civilised" candidate in meaningless elections lacking any positive vision.

In between, we'll be able to sleep in the safe embrace of global capitalism with a human face. The obscenity of the situation is breath-taking: global capitalism is now presenting itself as the last protection against fascism, and if you try to point this out you are accused of *complicity* with fascism.

Today's panicky anti-fascism doesn't bring hope, it kills hope—the hope that we'll really get rid of the threat of racist populism.

Like the Radicals of the 1960s, Antifa Groups Will Fade Into Irrelevancy

Sean Sullivan

Sean Sullivan is a freelance writer who has written for various publications, including Plurality Press, ArtBeat Magazine, Rooster Magazine, *and IdeaFrequency.com.*

At some point, every generation looks around and thinks they're living the dream of a paranoid schizophrenic. Nothing makes sense. Flames lick the corners of society, while rationality, love and tolerance sink closer to the black hole at the center of a dying earth's heart. Welcome to 2017. A time where flying cars, replicators and Star Trek's Data studying for the Turing Test were supposed to exist; instead, we have a polarized political climate that routinely escalates into YouTube videos of violence—because having the loudest voice in the arena isn't enough to feel like you're right anymore.

Which brings us to Antifa (or "anti-fascist), a loosely knit affiliation of left-wing activists who protest—what they categorize as—fascist demonstrations. While Antifa has been prominent in one form or another in European countries like Germany for over 60 years, the group has gained traction in the United States since the election of Donald Trump.

You know when Antifa is around. They dress using black bloc tactics, wear black hoodies and dark sunglasses, scarves and masks, turning the choreographed group into a nebulous, ominous blob. One news story after another has marked them with an indelible strain of violence, at Berkeley, Portland, and most recently, Evergreen State College in Olympia, Washington.

What the hell is going on?

"I think we're in a time when we can't ignore the extremism

"Antifa: Inside the Controversial Politics of a Supremely Violent Alt-left," by Sean Sullivan, Rooster Magazine, June 23, 2017. Reprinted with permission.

from the left," said Oren Segal, director of the Center on Extremism at the Anti-Defamation League (ADL) in a talk with Vice. He went on to say, "When we have anti-fascist counterprotests—not that they are the same as white supremacists—hat can ratchet up the violence at these events, and it means we can see people who are violent on their own be attracted to that. I hate to say it, but it feels inevitable."

Arguably the most notorious incident occurred recently in Berkeley, California, when an Antifa protestor pushed his way through a crowd and smashed an apparent Trump supporter's cranium with a bike lock. You can hear the crunch. Most terrifying isn't the senseless violent act, but the identity of the attacker: a philosophy professor who once taught ethics at Diablo Valley College in California. He's now in custody, being held on a $200,000 bail.

This isn't to say that right-leaning groups are devoid of violence. The ADL's senior research fellow at the Center on Extremism, Mark Pitcavage, told NPR, "In the past 10 years, when you look at murders committed by domestic extremists in the United States of all types, right-wing extremists are responsible for about 74 percent of those murders." But now it appears that the left is dusting off its 1971 copy of "The Anarchist Cookbook" and taking to the streets.

But why?

We tried contacting members of a local Antifa branch to understand their motivations, their end goal. Unfortunately, Antifa doesn't engage with the media, we were told, however they do often reveal themselves on various forums and through social media channels.

A glance is enough to confirm that Antifa's shorthand name is appropriate. They're worried that Nazis and White Nationalist—slumped together under the banners of fascism or the alt-right—have become empowered thanks to the Trump presidency, and are parading through communities to espouse and propagate hate.

"Antifa isn't there because some libertarians or republicans are gathering together to talk about how awesome capitalism is," writes choppinlefty on Reddit's Anarchism board. "Antifa is there because there are actual Nazis and white nationalists in your midst who pose a real threat to everyone, yourself included." They're convinced that a monster has rooted its tentacles in our soil.

That oddball word, "fascism," roughly refers to an extreme-right authoritarian government that favors group conformity over individuality, and utilizes violence to suppress opposing points of view. Not a nice system to live in.

Antifa can be described as a reactionary movement that is fearful a country is spiraling out of control. But that's a surface level reading. It doesn't explain a professor's logic to use unprovoked violence against a man wearing a sriracha hot sauce T-shirt. We have to go deeper. What is Antifa's political philosophy?

"My purpose in life is to help abolish the imperialist white supremacist capitalist heteropatriarchy," writes Donblon12—quite the direful sounding 21 syllable concept.

Donblon12 is espousing the real heart of Antifa. They're not just anti-fascist, but anti-status quo. They feel that they're suffering under the weight of an increasingly totalitarian state government that has brainwashed its citizens à la John Carpenter's "They Live." It seems "The greatest trick the [imperialist white supremacist capitalist heteropatriarchy] ever pulled was convincing the world he didn't exist."

Another commentator named theroyaltymustdie offers a further succinct explanation in a post titled "Listening to my conservative dad give career advice to my young professional sister..." in which he writes: "F*ck careers. F*ck the rat race. F*ck your internship and networking. F*ck your commodification of yourself. F*ck your celebration of working 75 hour weeks to please a gigantic corporation that doesn't give a single sh*t about you:"

No wonder then that Antifa is sympathetic towards socialism, Marxism, but especially some flavor of anarchism (particularly anarcho-communism). The fruition of such ideas is rarely elucidated or criticized within discussions, except as a link to an extensive FAQ, The Anarchist Library or the latest book by Peter Gelderloos.

Maybe these alternative viewpoints hold merit. Capitalism is not a perfect system—even the beaming free market economist Milton Friedman agreed (he happened to say something like "It's the best we've got for now.")—and perhaps continued socioeconomic change, and the birth of a genius or two, will gestate new ways of organizing that improve people's quality of life. Time marches on and reveals all.

But any value within Antifa's criticisms and propositions is perpetually eclipsed by conversations about violence, about the entrenched necessity of violence, about the spirit and efficacy of former violent revolutions.

Not everyone can string the syntax necessary to convey why violence is justified. But Antifa has media outlets like *It's Going Down* to serve as one of its intellectual spines. There, readers can find news, editorials and journals espousing the anti-fascist world view. While some articles are ambiguous about their stance on violence, others are outright explicit.

One of the webzines titled *Dangerous Spaces* opens with, "There is a violence that liberates. It is the murdered homophobe. It is the knee-capped rapist. It is the arson and the mink liberation. It is the smashed window and the expropriated food. It is the cop on fire and the riot behind bars. It is work avoidance, squatting, criminal friendship, and the total refusal of compromise. It is the chaos that can never be stopped."

The introduction concludes with, "We hope this publication can contribute in some way to a gender strike that will burn this world to the ground. Until the last rapist is hung with the guts of the last frat boy."

While there are likely Antifa members who have a highlighted copy of Leo Tolstoy's "The Kingdom of God Is Within You" on their bookshelf, those with pacifistic leanings seem to be an increasing minority. Peace is dead: "A timely reminder. There should be no tolerance and no quarter extended for those who seek to destroy us." Insulated Antifa media channels propagate a zero-sum game that reads like the denouement of the end of the world.

Even Vice has given voice to violence in an article titled "All I'm Saying Is, Give Violence a Chance," which says, "Could violence, in some way, improve our vain (in both senses of the word) attempts to fix our country?"

While the contents of the article don't form a rallying cry to pick up a sledgehammer, there is enough support to reinforce people's biases—because people don't read articles. They often only read clickbait headlines and then reinforce their secluded perspectives. The author, Josh Androsky, is a disgusting dilettante: perverting John Lennon's legacy with spittle from the excretion of a lobotomized ameba.

"It is refreshing to see a non-pacifist article. I feel like too many anarchists fall into this feel-good non-violent philosophy that is not at all commonsensical," praises blinkyblonky in response to Vice's article. He adds. "It may be a form of protest and change, but real change takes action, violent if necessary. If you want to stage sit-downs, marches within the permitted areas, all causing no disruption whatsoever, and expect to come out the victor, I'm sorry but I just don't see how any of that will change anything in the type of dramatic way the world society needs."

It's an *Us vs. The World* attitude that's propagating like the death-bleaching of coral reefs. Or we can better reframe it as an internalized good versus evil mythology: that Antifa believes they're on the right side of history—a phrase which ought to terrify as any action can be justified to achieve an end when one assumes the historical moral high ground.

Antifa considers themselves freedom fighters. "What we do know is that we need a dynamic, fighting, and combative movement," reads an *It's Going Down* article from December "We need networks of defense, support, and offensive capacity that can not only fight in the struggles that lay all around us but can begin to build new worlds."

After each violent incident—and there will be more—there's an outright, adamant refusal to condemn one's own actions in favor of justifying lex talionis (the Babylonian Code of Hammurabi which is known as an "eye for an eye"). Instead violence against others is laughed at, applauded, cherished. With Antifa it culminates most clearly in comics and memes like the Punch a Nazi meme. "If they're Nazis, it's morally acceptable to punch them."

Nobody, as far as I can tell, asks anymore, "Does violence work?"

Violence has become axiomatic because the society at large is perceived as violent. Here, we have further evidence for the epiphany that many adolescents never transition to adulthood. They become oversized children with legal rights who are better equipped to make excuses for their actions by playing with abstract semantics.

Here's an example. In response to the Alexandria shooting *It's Going Down* published an article that reads, "In perpetuating an unbearable status quo, the authorities are ensuring that men like Hodgkinson have nothing to lose." So, Hodgkinson is but one gear propelled by a system equally at fault. The article goes on to say:

"Bernie Sanders is missing the point when he decries the violence of Hodgkinson's attack and argues that only nonviolent activity can bring about social change. There are no hierarchies without violence; accepting a hierarchical social order means accepting and legitimizing violence as a fundamental aspect of our society. The question is not whether to be violent or not, but how to bring about the end of this social order."

That's why there are threads advising Antifa members to learn how to handle themselves in violent situations; and others that sprout up after incidents like the Berkeley protests in which Antifa members called for action to learn how to wield firearms and to head to protests bearing weapons. Drep_Reaper writes, "A shocking number of our comrades went in there with absolute no combat training. We need to set up seminars or something of the sort." (Yes, they refer to each other as "comrades.")

"We need to take notes from the John Brown Gun Club and get firearms and training." says The_Great_Cornlord. "I know getting firearms in states and cities we have a presence in is usually a hassle, but even handguns would help. It would certainly put a psychological element in while holding fash back [sic]. Who do you think a fascist is more afraid of? People with only flags and bats, or people with flags, bats, and guns?" When the first gun is brandished, be assured, chaos will reign.

Clearly, Antifa is scared and angry, like a bonobo backed into a corner while snakes slither from every angle. Cortisol kicks in and irrationality in the name of half-baked ideology takes charge. Unchecked emotion combined with naivety is what gives rise to appalling consequences, as it has in every civilization.

History serves a valuable lesson here in the vein of Robespierre, who reigned terror on France in the wake of the Revolution. Anyone who was even suspected of holding counter-views was murdered. If Antifa ushered in the revolution tomorrow would they wheel out the guillotine along with it? After all, the guillotine provides an irrefutable argument.

But when it comes to Antifa, horror won't be perpetrated by the group. Atrocities will be perpetrated by impressionable individuals.

If a person is inundated with the grandiloquent gestures of an oppressive world, day-after-day from behind their LCD monitor, chewing until propaganda is stuck to their mandibles, how long until they snap? It's the lone wolf—the person sunk into anihilistic despair who has given up on a meaningful existence within the current socioeconomic order that wants to inflict as much harm as possible before turning the gun on himself—who we should fear.

How long until someone dies at one of these protests?

As an outside observer, it's impossible not to feel like Jane Goodall, who experienced an inner tragedy when she witnessed the once peaceful chimps she loved fracture into tribes and rip each other apart limb by limb for four years. We're regressing.

People used to have patient and erudite debates. What happened? It's apt to remember that we're almost genetically identical to our primate cousins.

Are there injustices in the world? Are their abuses of power and cheaters and racists and White Supremacists and people who celebrate Hitler, whose voices ought never be allowed to speak alone? Of course, there are. There always will be, too.

But to confront those oppositional views with violence only gives more power to them, only discredits personal views. Nobody cares to understand a Utopian flavor of anti-fascist anarchism when actions speak louder than words, as they always have. When a woman stabs a police horse with a flag embedded with a silver nail, an entire movement is condemned to hell. They inspire fear, and nobody looking through the window feels sorry for them.

It's not propaganda by the right that's ostracized Antifa. It's their own actions. It's the webzines that call for slitting the throats of fascists that make Antifa a synonym for "violence."

Why not encapsulate the virtues of the future it proposes—the autonomous sisterhood and brotherhood humanitarian Golden Age—instead of orbiting a dead planet? If the rebuttal is that the media will not give Antifa the time of day, then so be it. But of course there is always an intellect willing to defend an outrageous viewpoint, so why question the strategy?

Why? Because right now Antifa looks as abhorrent and dictatorial as the very fascists they claim to oppose.

It's impossible to project where these extreme political cadres on both the left and right are headed, though the Sixties offers some parallels. The groups fade into irrelevancy with time, as political and social circumstances naturally morph, and breed new conflicts. Almost always. Then again, sometimes something persists, like a virus hanging on to an asteroid hurtling through the endless void of space. Eventually, it hits Earth and leaves a mysterious crater in Tunguska.

Yet as far as anyone can tell, the Antifa of today would celebrate the apocalypse and build a gulag in its heart.

Organizations to Contact

The editors have compiled the following list of organizations concerned with the issues debated in this book. The descriptions are derived from materials provided by the organizations. All have publications or information available for interested readers. This list was compiled on the date of publication of the present volume; the information provided here may change. Be aware that many organizations take several weeks or longer to respond to inquiries, so allow as much time as possible.

American Civil Liberties Union (ACLU)
125 Broad Street, 18th Floor
New York, NY 10004
phone: (212) 549-2500
website: www.aclu.org

For nearly 100 years, the ACLU has been the nation's guardian of liberty, working in courts, legislatures, and communities to defend and preserve the individual rights and liberties that the Constitution and the laws of the United States guarantee everyone in this country.

The Centrist Project
2420 17th Street, 3rd Floor
Denver, CO 80202
phone: (703) 962-1354
email: campaign@centristproject.org
website: www.centristproject.org

The Centrist Project is a grassroots organization dedicated to organizing Centrist Americans, supporting Centrist policies, and encouraging more independent candidates to run for public office to put the country ahead of any political faction in order to solve problems.

Convergence Center for Policy Resolution

1133 19th Street, NW
Suite 410
Washington, DC 20036
phone: (202) 830-2310
email: info@convergencepolicy.org
website: www.convergencepolicy.org

Convergence Center for Policy Resolution is a nonprofit organization focused on solving social challenges through collaboration. The Convergence team brings deep knowledge of policy and process and works with leaders and doers to move past divergent views to identify workable solutions to seemingly intractable issues.

Democratic National Committee (DNC)

430 South Capitol Street, SE
Washington, DC 20003
phone: (202) 863-8000
website: www.democrats.org

Since 1848, the Democratic National Committee has been the home of the Democratic Party, the oldest continuing party in the United States.

FactCheck.org

Annenberg Public Policy Center
202 South 36th Street
Philadelphia, PA 19104-3806
phone: (215) 898-9400
email: editor@factcheck.org
website: www.factcheck.org

FactCheck.org is a nonpartisan, nonprofit "consumer advocate" for voters that aims to reduce the level of deception and confusion in US politics. They monitor the factual accuracy of what is said by major US political players in the form of TV ads, debates, speeches, interviews, and news releases.

It's Going Down (IGD)
email: protonmail@itsgoingdown.org
website: itsgoingdown.org

IGD is a digital community center for anarchist, anti-fascist, autonomous anti-capitalist and anti-colonial movements. Their stated mission is to provide a resilient platform to publicize and promote revolutionary theory and action. They publish news related to anarchism and anti-fascism along with original content, anonymous submissions, and repost articles from websites with a similar perspective.

Pew Research Center
1615 L Street, NW
Suite 800
Washington, DC 20003
phone: (202) 419-4300
website: www.pewresearch.org

Pew Research Center is a nonpartisan fact tank that informs the public about the issues, attitudes, and trends shaping the world. It conducts public opinion polling, demographic research, media content analysis, and other empirical social science research. Pew Research Center does not take policy positions.

PolitiFact
1100 Connecticut Avenue, NW
Suite 440
Washington, DC 20036
phone: (202) 463-0571
website: www.politifact.com

PolitiFact is a fact-checking website that rates the accuracy of claims by elected officials and others who speak up in American politics.

Republican National Committee (RNC)
310 First Street, SE
Washington, DC 20003
phone: (202) 863-8500
website: www.gop.com

The Republican National Committee is a US political committee that provides national leadership for the Republican Party of the United States.

Southern Poverty Law Center
400 Washington Avenue
Montgomery, AL 36104
phone: (334) 956-8200
website: www.splcenter.org

Southern Poverty Law Center is a research organization that monitors hate groups and other extremists throughout the US and exposes their activities to law enforcement agencies, the media, and the public.

United States Institute of Peace (USIP)
2301 Constitution Avenue, NW
Washington, DC 20037
phone: (202) 457-1700
website: www.usip.org

USIP is America's nonpartisan institute to promote national security and global stability by reducing violent conflicts abroad. Their staff guide peace talks and advise governments, train police and religious leaders, and support community groups opposing extremism—all to help troubled countries solve their own conflicts peacefully.

Bibliography

Books

Madeleine Albright. *Fascism: A Warning.* New York, NY: HarperCollins, 2018.

Sigal R. Ben-Porath. *Free Speech on Campus.* Philadelphia, PA: University of Pennsylvania Press, 2017.

Mark Bray. *Antifa: The Anti-Fascist Handbook.* New York, NY: Melville House Publishing, 2017.

Ian Bremmer. *Us vs. Them: The Failure of Globalism.* New York, NY: Penguin Random House, 2018.

Shane Burley. *Fascism Today: What It Is and How to Fight It.* Oakland, CA: AK Press, 2017.

William A. Galston. *Anti-Pluralism: The Populist Threat to Liberal Democracy.* New Haven, CT: Yale University Press, 2018.

Scott Greer. *No Campus for White Men: The Transformation of Higher Education into Hateful Indoctrination.* Washington, DC: WND Books, 2017.

Thomas E. Mann and Norman J. Ornstein. *It's Even Worse Than It Looks: How the American Constitutional System Collided with the New Politics of Extremism.* Philadelphia, PA: Basic Books, 2012.

Jon Meacham. *The Soul of America: The Battle for Our Better Angels.* New York, NY: Random House, 2018.

Darren Mulloy. *American Extremism: History, Politics, and the Militia Movement (Routledge Studies in Extremism and Democracy).* New York, NY: Routledge. 2004.

David Neiwert. *Alt-America: The Rise of the Radical Right in the Age of Trump.* New York, NY: Verso, 2017.

Alexander Reed Ross. *Against the Fascist Creep*. Chico, CA: AK Press, 2017

Ben Shapiro. *Bullies: How the Left's Culture of Fear and Intimidation Silences Americans*. New York, NY: Simon & Schuster, 2013.

Timothy Snyder. *The Road to Unfreedom: Russia, Europe, America*. New York, NY: Tim Duggan Books, 2018.

Cass R. Sunstein, ed. *Can It Happen Here?: Authoritarianism in America*. New York, NY: HarperCollins, 2018.

Vegas Tenold. *Everything You Love Will Burn: Inside the Rebirth of White Nationalism in America*. New York, NY: Nation Books, 2018.

M. Testa. *Militant Anti-Fascism: A Hundred Years of Resistance*. Oakland, CA: AK Press, 2015.

Brad Todd and Salena Zito. *The Great Revolt: Inside the Populist Coalition Reshaping American Politics*. New York, NY: Crown Forum, 2018

Periodicals and Internet Sources

Stephanie Basile, "The Anti-Capitalist Politics of Antifa," *CounterPunch*, September 6, 2017. https://www.counterpunch.org/2017/09/06/the-anti-capitalist-politics-of-antifa/.

Peter Beinart, "The Rise of the Violent Left," *Atlantic*, September, 2017. https://www.theatlantic.com/magazine/archive/2017/09/the-rise-of-the-violent-left/534192/.

Russell Berman, "What's the Answer to Political Polarization in the US?" *Atlantic*, March 8, 2016. https://www.theatlantic.com/politics/archive/2016/03/whats-the-answer-to-political-polarization/470163/.

Mark Bray, "Who Are the Antifa?" *Washington Post*, August 16, 2017. https://www.washingtonpost.com/news/made-

by-history/wp/2017/08/16/who-are-the-antifa/?utm_
term=.1474a68bea2e.

Nate Cohn, "Polarization Is Dividing American Society, Not
Just Politics," *New York Times*, June 12, 2014. https://www.
nytimes.com/2014/06/12/upshot/polarization-is-dividing-
american-society-not-just-politics.html.

David French, "On Extremism, Left and White," *National Review*,
May 30, 2017. http://www.nationalreview.com/article/448108/
political-extremism-beleaguers-both-left-and-right.

Nicholas Goroff, "Letter to the American Left: Antifa Is Not
Your Friend," *Occupy Online*, February 28, 2017. https://
www.occupy.com/article/letter-american-left-antifa-not-
your-friend#sthash.bsj0vLxB.dpbs.

Joshua Hersh, "Extremism Experts Are Starting to Worry
About the Left," *Vice News*, June 15, 2017. https://news.vice.
com/en_ca/article/3kpeb9/extremism-experts-are-starting-
to-worry-about-the-left.

Sean Illing, "They Have No Allegiance to Liberal Democracy:
An Expert on Antifa Explains the Group," *Vox*, August 25,
2017. https://www.vox.com/2017/8/25/16189064/antifa-
charlottesville-activism-mark-bray-interview.

John Kass, "The Democratic Silence on Antifa Is Dangerous,"
Chicago Tribune, August 29, 2017. http://www.
chicagotribune.com/news/columnists/kass/ct-antifa-kass-
met-0830-20170829-column.html.

Ed Kilgore, "In the Trump Era, America Is Racing Toward Peak
Polarization," *New York Magazine*, May 31, 2017. http://
nymag.com/daily/intelligencer/2017/05/in-the-trump-era-
america-is-racing-toward-peak-polarization.html.

Kevin Mattson, "The Forgotten Roots of Antifa," *Democracy
Journal*, September 19, 2017. https://democracyjournal.org/
alcove/the-forgotten-roots-of-antifa/.

Casey Michel, "How Liberal Portland Became America's Most Politically Violent City," *Politico*, June 30, 2017. https://www.politico.com/magazine/story/2017/06/30/how-liberal-portland-became-americas-most-politically-violent-city-215322.

Pew Research Center, "Political Polarization, 1994-2017," Pew Research Center, October 20, 2017. http://www.people-press.org/interactives/political-polarization-1994-2017/.

Matthew Sheffield, "Anti-fascist Radicals: Liberals Don't Realize the Serious Danger of the Alt-Right," *Salon*, March 10, 2017. https://www.salon.com/2017/03/10/anti-fascist-radicals-liberals-dont-realize-the-serious-danger-of-the-alt-right/.

Index

R

racism, 16, 33, 55, 67, 73, 82, 86, 87,
    101, 121, 134
Republican Party/GOP, 35, 37, 50,
    98, 101, 102, 116, 119, 150, 151
right wing/far right extremism, 44,
    45, 53, 56, 81–84, 114, 116,
    118–126, 146, 155, 159, 160
Rimel, Logan, 123
Ross, Alexander Reid, 42, 43–44

S

Sanders, Bernie, 14, 76, 98, 163
Saunders, George, 47
skinheads, 33, 36, 42, 58, 86, 90, 114
Social Democratic Party (SPD),
    20–21, 22, 23, 25, 26, 147
social democrats, 19, 20, 27, 58, 59
Socialist Unity Party (SED), 22, 26,
    27, 28
social media, 53, 54, 55, 69, 71, 77,
    89, 159
Somerville, Frank, 67, 70
Southern Poverty Law Center,
    44–45, 87, 121, 136
Spencer, Richard B., 36, 37, 49, 51,
    55, 88, 102, 121
Stone, Arlo, 125–126

T

Testa, M., 87
Trotsky, Leon, 122
Trump, Donald, 16, 30, 35–36, 45,
    53, 56, 62, 68, 81, 85, 87–88,
    89, 90, 114, 115, 116, 118, 119,
    120, 132, 141, 146, 155, 158
authoritarian/fascist tendencies
    of, 14, 83, 93, 101, 104, 134,
    148, 149–150, 152
inauguration of, 37, 50, 55, 57, 91,
    92, 102
protests in opposition of, 40–41,
    42, 44, 47

rallies in support of, 39, 40, 41, 98,
    106, 111, 147

U

Unite the Right rally (Charlottesville,
    VA), 34, 35, 119

W

white nationalists, 16, 33, 53, 56, 57,
    68, 71, 88, 90, 100, 116, 126,
    131, 132, 159, 160
white supremacy and supremacists,
    14, 32, 33, 36, 37, 48, 50, 55,
    86, 90, 102, 111, 114–116, 118,
    119, 120, 121, 123, 141, 143,
    144, 146, 159
Women's March, 57, 91, 92, 96, 112
World War II, 33, 46, 54, 58, 82, 136,
    147

Y

Yiannopolous, Milo, 37, 41, 46–47,
    48, 49, 52, 57–58, 97, 101

Z

Zimmerman, Alan, 124